images of women
in Zimbabwean Literature

rudo b. gaidzanwa

The College Press

Cover Illustration by Gillian Wright

THE COLLEGE PRESS (PVT) LTD
P.O. Box 3041
Harare
Zimbabwe

©R.B. Gaidzanwa
First Published 1985

Printed by
LITHO SERVICES (PVT) LTD
Harare

ISBN 0 86925 584 3

No part of this publication may be reproduced, stored in a retrieval system, or transmitted in any form or by any means, electronic, mechanical, photocopying, recording or otherwise without the prior permission in writing of the publisher.

For Mama and Tata

Acknowledgements

I am greatly indebted to colleagues, friends and acquaintances for their help. Des Gasper discussed with me the images of tough women. Charles Mungoshi put me in touch with Jester at the Zimbabwe Publishing House. Dr Carolyn Clark, University of California, Santa Cruz, Mr R. Zinyemba and Dr Anthony Chennells from the Department of English at the University of Zimbabwe all advised usefully on various aspects of women's images in literature. Professor George Kahari from the Department of African Languages, University of Zimbabwe discussed the Shona novels with me. Tsitsi Dangarembga encouraged me in many ways. Other colleagues and acquaintances, too numerous to mention, helped to clarify concepts and issues at various levels of seriousness. I am grateful to all of them for their support.

Rejoice Maduapera, with the help of Jean Taylor, typed the manuscript of this book at a time when the Department of Sociology, University of Zimbabwe, was at its busiest, I sincerely thank them for their help.

	Page
Preface	7
Introduction	8
Women as mothers	14
Women as wives	29
Women without husbands	50
Rural and Urban women	67
Conclusion	87
Bibliography	100

Preface

This book examines the dominant images of black women presented in Shona, Ndebele and English literature by blacks in Zimbabwe. Most of the novels, collections of short stories and plays are written by black male authors in Zimbabwe. For the purposes of this book, six novels by women were selected in all three languages together with at least twelve other works by male authors. Most of the novels were written in the seventies with a few, particularly in English, written and published in 1980 or immediately after.

The reason for the different times of publication is that literature in English prior to Independence did not get published unless it could satisfy the censors that it was non-political. Thus, some of the works in English were banned and published only after Independence.

The images of women which are analysed and explored are those of mothers, wives, single, divorced and widowed women, rural and urban women. There are positive as well as negative images of women in the literature. However, there are differences in the way positively and negatively portrayed women are treated.

The introduction is historical and tries to explain the socio-economic, political and psychological bases for the portrayal of women in particular ways. It also considers the similarities and differences between male and female authors in the way they construct images of women. There is also a consideration of the ways in which some male authors have more positive images of women than some female authors.

The ways in which different authors view relationships between men, women and children are varied. There are similarities in the stereotyping of women's images while at the same time differences exist in the way the works written in English depict women. The works in English depart from the main body of Shona and Ndebele literature in that they are not heavily moralistic, condemning and punitive of female behaviour that deviates from the norm.

The settings of the novels, stories and plays range from the rural lands, farms, plantations and towns. Despite the diversity in location of the stories and plays there are consistences in the way women's roles and images are constructed and depicted.

This book deals with the images and their implications. It was a result of discussions and observations with many people on the subject of women's images in Zimbabwe. It will be well worth the effort if it stimulates more writing and discussion of works that will engender sensitive and positive portrayal of women in literature and other media.

Introduction

Before the independence of Zimbabwe, the issue of black women in society was overshadowed by other issues such as liberation of the whole nation from colonialism. During that time, the concerns of white women had more precedence because of the dominance of white people over the social, economic and political processes in colonised Zimbabwe.

A lot has been written about the perceptions of white people about black people in general and black women in particular. Writers like Doris Lessing have written about the way white colonials viewed black women. However, very little attention has been given to the way black authors writing in Shona, Ndebele and English have constructed images of black women in Zimbabwe. The views of black writers are very important because as formerly colonised people, it is interesting to examine the way they internalised and interpreted the experience of colonisation as reflected by the way they form images of women. Long after independence, it will be interesting to see if the way women are viewed will change to reflect the changed social and political order.

One could ask the question 'Why women's images?' Women's images are important because as the bulk of the rural, most materially disadvantaged sector of Zimbabwe's population, women have a major stake in encouraging and struggling for a more just order. The struggle for justice can be handicapped if women have a negative image in society. A negative image delegitimises their struggle for fundamental rights and freedoms such as the right to jobs, education, health and other valued goods and services in society.

Secondly, the way a society is constructed and the way it operates is of interest to sociologists, anthropologists, economists, political scientists and other social scientists whose interest it is to study dimensions of human behaviour in society. Zimbabwe has just undergone a war of liberation and this experience has changed the expectations and behaviour of most groups in society in Zimbabwe. Literature is an important part of this experience because it mirrors and interprets the experience from the points of view of those who write about it. It is also important to recognise that the struggles of women in Zimbabwe predate colonialism, continued throughout the colonial era and after independence. The emergence of the women's movement in the West, fuelled by the struggles of Third World peoples in Cuba, Vietnam and the struggles of Black and ethnic Americans, has helped to highlight the struggles of women in the Third World. In this connection, women, as substantial sections of Third World countries' populations are very important because of the kinds of experiences they undergo within largely male dominated societies. During revolutions and periods of social change, the rights and freedoms of the disadvantaged become focal issues. Similarly, the rights of women in the world have become focal issues becasue of the particular experiences of women.

From a sociological point of view, it is necessary to conduct a study of women's images in literature in Zimbabwe because it is desirable to determine whether these images approximate social reality. If they do not, it is interesting to determine why not and if they do, it is equally interesting to determine why and to what extent they do.

Criteria for the selection of the novels, plays and short stories

There was a purposive selection of the novels by the language categories. It was important to include a good number of Shona and Ndebele novels since Shona and Ndebele are the major languages in which most of the literate people express themselves and read for leisure. Works written in English by blacks were fewer and most of them were published after Independence.

Within the language categories, most writers are male. It was necessary to ensure that some female writers are represented in all language categories.

In the Shona and Ndebele langauges, some works that had been serialised on radio or used as set texts in schools were included. The reason was that a lot of people who are literate in Shona and Ndebele would be familiar with them. Other works that I had not read or heard of were included.

In the English language category, I chose the works of the better known writers such as Mungoshi, Marechera, Nyamfukudza and Makhalisa. Mungoshi had already been published in Shona and English before Independence. Two of his Shona works are also dealt with in this work. Makhalisa, a female author, had already published in Ndebele before Independence. Marechera was published by 1980 and had the honour of having one of his works banned in Zimbabwe. The appeal against the ban attracted interest and publicity. Nyamfukudza had a novel published by 1980, the year of Independence. All these works are popular and familiar to the section of the public that is literate in English.

The authors in Shona and Ndebele in this work are mostly better known ones. Sigogo, Chakaipa, Kuimba, Hamandishe, Tsodzo, Mukonoweshuro, Moyo, Khiyaza, Mlilo and Ngwenya have all had more than one novel published. Thus for most of the authors with more than one publication, I treated individual novels most of the time. The exception was Mungoshi who had only one of his volume of short stories analysed and two of his Shona novels included in this work. This was necessary because he is well known in Shona and English. His other works in English have been treated and analysed elsewhere while the short stories are relatively unexplored by critics. Makhalisa's works in Ndebele are not treated because they fall into the genre of the venacular writings and it is her short stories in English that offered new and more stimulating insights and analyses of her development as a writer.

★ ★ ★

Currently, there is a lot of debate about the role of women in society in Zimbabwe. To this end, the situations and representations of rural as well as urban women in literature have been examined and compared. From these images, people wishing to change society can glean information about social attitudes to women of all types and circumstances. For example, the Legal Age of Majority Act of 1982, confers majority on all Zimbabweans when they turn eighteen. This provision has caused alarm and concern on the part of parents of young women and husbands of women who were legal minors before the Act. The Act has a fundamental impact on relations between the sexes within the family and marriage. It changes the frame of reference for women's lives within the society to some extent and it is this fact that has discomfitted some people. Such an Act will necessarily alter women's images as reflected in literature. The direction and tone of this change still has to be determined.

At the same time, the images of women as presently portrayed need examination in terms of their sources, their veracity according to women's experiences, and their potential for positive transformation in the future. However, in this exercise, one cannot overlook the writers' own input in the characterisations of these women and the construction of their images. Obvious questions such as the writers' intentions, beliefs and values arise. There are instances where characters may be mutilated in order to make moral points. Such instances have been pinpointed in this book. There are other instances where the writers may also construct characters with the aim of changing society's view of women for better or worse. The writers' own conceptions and beliefs about women's place and role in Zimbabwean society have a lot of influence in determining the way characters act and react to certain situations. In the vernacular works examined, the aim is largely to point a moral and convey a powerful message about how society ought to be structured and how people ought to behave. This has been pointed out in connection with writers like Chakaipa, Sigogo, Kuimba, Ncube and other authors in this genre of writing.

What is of concern here is the basic assumption of women's nature and being as outlined in the writings. The more morally directed and didactic works also have a very traditional and conservative view of women's role and participation in society. They tend to be nostalgic and to stress how things used to be in the 'good old days'. In the context of Zimbabwe, the 'good old days' refer to the situation prevailing before colonisation. This was a pre-capitalist situation and it is when a renaissance of this period within a system of under-developed capitalism is attempted that controversy about what women's role in society should be arises. This attempt at rediscovering 'roots' can also be viewed from the other direction whereby authors may depict women in a liberated and unconventional way. This can be said of Mutize's *Mary Ponderai*. However, the latter stance also has its own assumptions and may pose its own problems. For example, the characterisation of Mary as a female gangster may give the impression that women only aspire to be equal to men in unsavoury pursuits and activities. It may also be revealing in that the author could be taken to be unable to conceive of women in a more credible and ordinary situation of liberation and role playing *vis avis* men. It may illustrate the fact that the role of women cannot be concretised on an everyday, ordinary and experiential level. The construction of images of women which are non-threatening, and safer because of their incredibility may be viewed as part of the process of insulating consumers of literature from the possibility of women's participation at a more routine and effective level in society.

From a sociological perspective, it is necessary to focus on the images of women as depicted in the literature. Women are depicted as mothers, wives, divorcees, widows, single, jilted and prostitute women. In most of the works considered, women are the major characters. This is sociologically significant because in a male dominated capitalist society, the women are not the most highly regarded. However, as the most powerless, black women are the subject of writers in much the same way that black people, their supposed behaviour, expectations and aspirations preoccupied white writers in white societies with subjugated black populations.

As mothers, women are expected to fulfil all their children's expectations. What children want influences the way they view their mothers. Children who approve of their mothers may be those whose mothers give them love, material things and affection. Conversely, those mothers whose interests do not suit their children may be viewed as cold, selfish and uncaring. This is particularly so in the relationships between mothers and sons. The needs of mothers for companionship, love and affection may be subordinated to the needs of the sons. When mothers look for other men who may not be the fathers of those sons for affection, sons do not generally approve of their mothers' actions. In a society like Zimbabwe, most men in rural areas are labour migrants and stay way from home and families for long periods on end. The men may actually start other families in towns. Thus the expectation of fidelity from sons and husbands is taxing on women in a way that it is not for men since men are not penalised for adultery as strictly as women are. Similarly, women whose husbands are weak or absent and thus unable to reinforce or enforce the expected mother role pay a heavy price since their children condemn them. *Ndochema Naani?* by Mandebvu depicts such a situation.

As wives, women are expected to behave in comforting, non-aggressive and nurturant ways. They are there to make life manageable for husbands and children. Wives are also expected to be faithful, both physically and socially to their husbands. When wives refuse to do so, they are disapproved of. In Zimbabwe, where most husbands are absent for long periods because of labour migrancy, this is a difficult role because wives then perform wifely social duties to husbands' lineages without the day to day supports and benefits that a physically present husband can give. In the literature, the bulk of the problem women are those who fall down on their wifely duties and responsibilities. These duties include bearing children, subordinating themselves to husbands, remaining faithful to the husbands and deferring to the husband's mother, father or other relations. Childless, domineering or assertive, unfaithful and insubordinate women are despised and socially disapproved.

Women who have no husbands and children are usually those who have refused to marry, been unsuccessful in maintaining marriages, widows, single or jilted women. Some of these women are depicted as beautiful and sexually attractive.

Their beauty is used as explanation for the failure of their marriages. Men are pardoned and largely condoned from responsibility for explaining or consorting with them against social expectation because these women are bewitching and irresistible. With most of these women's beauty goes moral decadence and corruption. In Shona, the proverb goes *Mukadzi munaku kurega kuroya anoba*, translating, 'A beautiful woman always has a blemish. If she is not a witch, she is a thief'. Similarly in Ndebele, there is a proverb *Akukho geza lingela siyinga* meaning that 'There is nobody who is perfect and beautiful people always have flaws of one sort or another'.

While women are enjoined to be beautiful and attractive in order to titillate men, they are also condemned for this role if they exploit it without necessarily becoming wives and mothers. In the vernacular works, when women use their beauty for their own material advantage, they are not approved of. They may get involved in affairs that lead to their death or moral destruction. If beauty or womanliness does not attract any man, then a woman without a husband must remain chaste and single. Like sister Ruth in Bepswa's *Ndakamuda Dakara Afa*, she may choose a higher cause like serving God but she must not use her body and wiles to attract and enjoy herself physically and materially with men who are not her husband. Once women choose to enter or are pushed into sexual liaisons with men they are not married to, they become prostitutes. There is no distinction made between lovers, mistresses, concubines and prostitutes. As long as a woman has sex with a man who is not her husband, she is held to be a prostitute, implicity or explicity.

Rural women are held in higher esteem than urban women. This is because rural women are more innocent and naive where the influences of urbanisation on behaviour and expectations are concerned. Rarely do women who have not been to town commit adultery. While rural women are put on a pedestal, they are also sinned against more greviously by men than their urban counterparts. Part of rural women's innocence is their inability to rebel against or repay their men for actual insult or injury suffered. This martyr role of rural women as injured but innocent makes them ideal wives and mothers. The fact that the husbands of these women eventually come back to the wives, tired of sin and repentant, is supposed to illustrate to the wives the virtues of perseverance and subordination to one's husband.

On the other hand, women in towns or other semi-urban environments suffer greviously when they do not behave like decent wives and mothers. They die violently, get maimed or diseased and generally live tormented lives if they survive. These images discourage women from questioning the stereotypes and expectations placed on them. The women who step out of line suffer so much that it is not worth the trouble to rebel or question the social order.

This is the message communicated to urban women and others who aspire to be like them.

The reality of life, the economy and polity make such stereotype lives impossible even for women in rural areas. Rural women's diminishing incomes force them to be less accommodating to affinal relations. Resources are limited and need to be spent on one's own children. Caring for husband's parents and relations is very taxing for a poor couple. Under such circumstances, it is quite difficult to be generous to all. The expectations of rural women were raised by the liberation war and their participation in it. Their role was very crucial and it was recognised and appreciated. To expect them to lay aside their added knowledge, courage and increased awareness of the possibility of a more liberated, just and egalitarian life is both unrealistic and unfair.

In the end, it is more important to interpret the extent to which the women characterised in these works exploit their opportunities and potentialities to the full. It is not so much that a woman becomes a doctor, social worker, gangster, witch or prostitute. The kinds of calculations and choices a woman creates are the mark of liberation and freedom. This process entails understanding oneself and one's environment in a way that makes it possible to master one's life more meaningfully.

1

Women as mothers

Mothers and sons

The image of women as mothers is a dominant one in literature in Zimbabwe. Motherhood is respectable and held in high esteem as long as it goes with or is preceded by socially approved wifehood. In most of the books analysed in this study, the image of the mother, whatever her age, looms very large. However, the characterisation of mothers differs a great deal, ranging from unreasonable, evil, fearsome, to beloved and comforting ones.

There is a marked difference in the way mothers are perceived by their sons as opposed to their daughters. Sons who are young and unmarried often view their mothers with admiration and fear. This is exemplified by Stanley Nyamfukudza's story 'Crossing the river' in *Aftermaths*. The son sees his mother as a fearsome woman. He says 'her laugh carried so much disdain that you knew nothing you said would make any difference with her'.[1] He describes the way the veins in her neck stuck out when she was shouting and arguing with the bus conductor. He is afraid and ashamed of her. Her image is that of a determined but unreasonable woman. She braves the rain in order to take the family to town for Christmas. She does this to fulfil her boast to the other village women whom she had told that she and her children would spend Christmas away from the village. She is unreasonable in that she wants to take her children and herself across a flooded river on a footbridge.

She has a tender spot though and we glimpse this when she talks to her son. When she 'wins' her 'bet' against the bus conductor, the son is proud of her and admires her will and courage. 'After all we had crossed the river',[2] he crows to himself. Thus we can understand the mixed feelings the boy feels for his mother. He is afraid, embarrassed, as well as proud and pleased with her. He has a specific expectation about how mothers and women should behave. When his mother insists on taking them to town and crossing the flooded river, he sees her as undermining the role expected of her. After she has acted out of the expected role, he then admires and respects her for her success in breaking out of the role.

In Charles Mungoshi's story 'Who will stop the dark?' in *Some Kind of Wounds*, the mother is depicted as a tough, fearsome character. It is intimated to the reader that the mother had something to do with the maiming of the boy's father. She is depicted as mocking and biting in her talk. Her mouth is described as being ' . . . wrinkled tightly into an obscene little hole that reminded the boy of a cow's behind after dropping its dung'.[3] She is capable of silencing the boy with her eye. To the boy, the mother is a spoilsport who would stop him doing all the things he enjoys—things such as hunting mice and listening to his paternal grandfather's stories during schooltime. The boy, Zakeo, takes refuge at his grandfather's and tells him about all the things other boys say about his father. They say his father is his mother's horse, that his mother is a witch. The grandfather abets the boy in his truancy from school and the mother strops the boy for this. When the father tries to stop her beating the boy, he too gets stropped. She throws away the mice the boy has brought as a peace offering after spending the day away from school.

The mother is not altogether without redemption. She pleads with the boy's grandfather to let the boy go to school without the distraction of mouse trapping, fishing and other activities the old man liked to do with the boy during school time. She is hurt by the fact that the boy will not listen to her. She reminds the old man that the boy is the only child she has and the old man should not abet him in destroying his future. Her anguish is real and she walks away without any assurance that the old man will not take the boy on hunting and fishing expeditions when he ought to be at school. The boy's truancy from school continues with the complicity of the grandfather. The mother is frustrated and confused by the old man's complicity in the boy's disobedience. She strops the boy and starts crying herself, asking the boy why he is causing her all that suffering. She hugs him and tells him that she cares for him more than anybody else. He refuses to be touched by her tears and hugs. He tells her 'You don't know anything', the way his paternal grandfather said it of his classmates when they said the boy's mother was a witch who rode hyenas and his father. The boy walks off to his grandfather who knows that the boy has been stropped. The old man confuses the boy by telling him that one day he would realise that his mother had been right about the need for him to go to school. Thus even while the boy and his grandfather resent the mother, the grandfather knows she is right and that in future the boy would go to school possibly with the persuasion of the grandfather.

In Marechera's *The House of Hunger*, the mother is portrayed as a fearsome woman who beats her son for speaking to her in English. She also thrashes her two sons and their father for coming home drunk after which she chucks out the father for the whole night. The mother is feared rather than respected. She is very insensitive and crude towards her son, telling him to go to bed with girls instead of messing up the sheets with his masturbation. She does not care that she is embarrassing her son immensely.

It must be stated that Marechera treats all his characters with contempt and sarcasm. Even when he outlines the vulgarity of the mother's behaviour in *The House of Hunger* he is not specifically selective of her as a mother and as a woman. He has contempt for the sons, Peter and his brother, the husband who beats and sexually subdues his wife in public and other male characters. In fact, the mother cannot be otherwise if she is to survive in her household of brutalised people.

This tension between sons and mothers is also evident in Shona and Ndebele literature in Zimbabwe. In *Kutheni* by Eunice Mthethwa, Ntongenhle asks his mother why she and his father object to his intention to marry Ntombiye Hlazo. His mother MaMthombeni tells him that Msilawenja, Ntombi's father is not a good man and is rumoured to have murdered Masuku's daughter. Msilawenja also beat his wife Mabhena to death after she had protested over the affair between the Masuku girl, whom he is said to have murdered, and Msilawenja. MaMthombeni tells her son 'Indoda phela yinja'[4] (A man is like a dog). During the family discussion of Ntonga's marriage intentions, Ntonga protests that he is not marrying her family or clan and tells his parents that when Ntombi is his wife, she will do what he wants. MaMthombeni later comes round to her son's way of thinking when she discovers that Ntombi is a church goer and cannot be held responsible for her father's misdeeds. Thus MaMthombeni and her son's interests coincide despite her earlier misgivings about his choice of woman as a wife. Ntonga's father is adamant in his opposition to this choice. Later when the relationship between married sons and mothers is discussed, the attitude of Ntonga's mother to him will be re-examined.

In *Umzenzi Kakhalelwa* by Lenah Mazibuko, MaSibanda, the mother in the novel, has a strained relationship with her sons, both married and unmarried. The unmarried son of MaSibanda, Phathisani, openly criticises his mother for refusing to go to a diviner to find out what caused the death of Themba, his elder brother's son with MaNdlovu. Phathisani asks why, if prayers are so powerful, Themba died without any illness. Phathisani and Mloyiswa resent the fact that their mother neglects their father in favour of her church activities. Phathisani thinks his mother is a bit disturbed and that she henpecks their father. He supports the move by Mloyiswa and MaNdlovu away from their paternal home so as to verify the cause of MaNdlovu's misfortunes over her children who die in infancy. MaSibanda resents the fact that Mloyiswa only writes to Phathisani to inform him about how MaNdlovu and himself are getting on in Nkayi. Phathisani does not inform his parents that he is going to the University in Salisbury. Phathisani only goes home to his parents when it is reported by Mathe, a neighbour, that his father is seriously ill. Phathisani and his brother go home and find their father ill and on his own while their mother is holding a prayer meeting. MaSibanda tries to feed her sons a portion that will still their wrath against her but Deliwe, her daughter, unwittingly feeds the uneaten food to the dog, Bazangenzani (What will they do to me?). It turns out that MaSibanda is a witch and has a hand in her husband's illness. Phathisani had seen his mother carrying out suspicious activities at dawn and has overheard her conversation with MaNkiwane when they were arguing over who would feed the familiars kept in MaSibanda's granary. MaSibanda is depicted as a bully, a witch and an obstinate mother who is hated by her children. Unlike in the other stories and novels quoted before, she is not admired by her son, Phathisani who is not married. Like Zakeo in Mungoshi's story, 'Who will stop the dark?', MaSibanda is resented by Phathisani for her bad treatment of his father. Unlike Zakeo's mother, MaSibanda is not right even at the end. She is just evil as a mother whereas the other mothers are resented for being disciplinarians, strict and unbending especially when they are convinced they are right. MaSibanda is not loving even when she is going contrary to her son's wishes. Her image as a mother, and relationship to an unmarried son is quite unusual in its being almost totally negative.

In *Ngiphilelani* by Geshom Khiyaza, the relationship between MaDube and Thembeni her son is explored. MaDube spoils Thembeni in preference to her stepchildren. Thembeni is loved by his mother so much that he gets the best food, clothes and attention. Thembeni accepts and exploits his mother's love for him by lording it over his step brother and sister. He grows up an irresponsible boy and lands up in jail for taking part in the murder of a man who turns out to be his father. Later he blinds, in one eye, an elderly woman, who turns out to be his mother while trying to rob her of some money. MaDube is depicted as a misguided indulgent mother who spoils her son while treating her step-children badly. Her relationship with Thembeni is easy and relaxed as long as she panders to his whims but when she starts berating him for some of his misdeeds, he tells her off. Thembeni eventually gets expelled from school, gets into bad ways, helps in the robbery and murder of his father and the robbery of his mother. When he is sentenced, she tries to intervene and asks the court to release her son to her so that she can instruct him into good ways like all parents do their children. The court refuses her request on the grounds that he had shown no remorse and had gone back to his criminal ways after being pardoned from jail while serving the sentence for the murder of his father. In any case, the court asserted, how could she talk about instructing him at his age? He is sentenced to life imprisonment. Even then, Thembeni still blames his mother for bringing him up the way she did. He blames her for spoiling him while she thought she was only demonstrating her love for him. At the end, MaDube blames mothers for ruining their children's lives by spoiling them. Ultimately, Thembeni is absolved from much of the responsibility for his life since MaDube is portrayed as the major culprit in the ruination of her son. MaDube's relationship with Thembeni is finally servered by his imprisonment for life and she has to live the rest of her life in her stepson's home, a one-eyed, disillusioned and remorseful old woman.

In *Ndochema Naani?* by Stella Mandebvu, another dimension of the relationship between mothers and unmarried sons emerges. Munhamo (In trouble) and her son Mubayiwa have a good and loving relationship initially. However, this relationship gets strained after Mubayiwa's father dies. Mubayiwa starts analysing his mother's motivation and attitude towards him when she mentions that should he marry a wife, the wife would stop him from bringing his mother meat as he has done that day. Munhamo is depicted as a greedy and jealous woman and mother.

Mubayiwa decides to go to town to seek a waged job. His mother is not enthusiastic about the idea since she is afraid that anything might happen to her only son in town. Mubayiwa had heard rumours from neighbours to the effect that his mother had killed his father. He did not believe any of these rumours and is actually worried about leaving his mother and sisters since he loves them very much. Mubayiwa leaves for Gweru and, on his way, he meets Zimwai, who tells him about some widowed woman with whom he is having an affair.

Mubayiwa's relationship with his mother deteriorates further when his mother's involvement with Zimwai continues. He finally asks his mother what her relationship with Zimwai is. She tries to cover it up but it becomes clear that he is her lover as rumoured as far as Gweru where Mubayiwa has heard about it. Munhamo starts hating her son for having discovered her affair. Meanwhile Zimwai has made Munhamo's daughter Vimbai pregnant by raping her on one of the many occasions when her mother sent her on an errand to Zimwai's home. Mubayiwa finally discovers the complicity of his mother in the poisoning of his father. He also discovers that his mother's affair has led to the rape of Vimbai by Zimwai, and caused Vimbai's suicide. Munhamo is tried for poisoning her husband and she is sentenced to death. The death sentence severs Mubayiwa and his mother's relationship. Munhamo comes off as a cruel and unfaithful woman. Her relationship with her son is strained partly because of her son's sense of grievance over his father's death. This dimension of mother/son tension over the father is also evident in Mazibuko's *Umzenzi Kakhalelwa*, and Mungoshi's story 'Who will stop the dark?', discussed before. This strain is also evident in Chakaipa's *Pfumo Reropa* where Tanganeropa's relationship with his mother gets strained when he discovers that she is having an association, albeit unwillingly, with the tyrant Chief Nyadire who killed his father.

Mothers and young unmarried sons have varying relationships. When the sons are very young, they fear and admire their mothers' disciplinarian roles especially when the fathers are absent due to labour migracy or when the fathers are weak for other reasons such as disability. The mothers are strong characters who loom large in their son's lives and this raises mixed feelings in the sons on different occasions and situations. However, when the fathers are present, the sons seem to have closer and more loving relationships with their mothers while the fathers take on the disciplinarian roles.

Where the fathers are weak, absent or dead, the relationships between mothers and sons are strained. This results in jealousy on the son's side and a sense of grievance against the mothers especially if the sons construe the father's absence, weakness, or death to be due to the mother's actions. Where mothers have to compete with other women and their children as happens in polygamous or step-parent situations, mothers tend to be very protective and close to their children in general. Thus mothers and sons may be very close if the husband and father has other wives and sons who are competitors for the inheritance of property or when the mothers have to care for a divorced or deceased wife's children with their present husband. In such situations mothers try to gain material advantage for their sons against the claims of other women's sons. In such situations, mothers are portrayed as indulgent and passionately possessive to the extent that they pamper and spoil the sons. In non-competitive situations, the mothers are depicted as strong and firm, feared and admired as long as they try to get the best for their sons in the way of schooling and other material benefits. However, when the mothers start pursuing their personal interests and inclinations e.g. religion, lovers, etc., as opposed to those activities that directly benefit their children, conflict with the sons begins. In such instances, the mothers are portrayed as harming other people such as husbands, children and neighbours. The punishment for these women is usually very drastic. This may take the form of death, life imprisonment, extreme remorse, disability and destitution.

With married sons, the mother-son relationship is more complex. As mothers to married sons, various images of mothers prevail. In Mungoshi's 'The Victim' in *Some Kinds of Wounds*, Mangazva's mother is extremely influential and domineering over her son. Mangazva is afraid of his mother and fears her disapproval. He intimates to Mr Moyo that his mother pushed him into marrying. The mother occupies the most comfortable seat in the house, she greets her son, who is married and living with his wife, with a scolding. Her son shows his wounds incurred in a fight to her and not to his wife. 'Feel here, mother. You feel the bump?—Do you feel the bruises mother? Do you feel them mother?—'5 asks Mangazva of his mother while his wife is cowed into silence by his rebuke. His mother overrules her daughter-in-law over what Mangazva has to do if he is drunk, namely, to spend the night wherever he may be and avoid injury. His mother overrules that suggestion. His wife tells Mr Moyo that her husband sleeps in a room close to his parents while she sleeps with the children in one of the little huts. The mother here is a domineering women who continues to lay down the law for her married son and his wife. There is no overt conflict between mother and son because the son is very dependent on the mother. The mother overshadows the father of Mangazva whom she has called a barking dog and a castrated bull, by inference, in a cryptic rejoinder to the father's rebuke of Mangazva.

In Mazibuko's *Umzenzi Kakhalelwa* MaSibanda the mother has already been shown to have been in conflict with her sons. However, with Mloyiswa her elder son, the conflict is heightened by the fact that his children with MaNdlovu continue to die in infancy under suspicious circumstances. Mloyiswa also resents his mother's excessive devotion to her church while she neglects her husband. Mloyiswa eventually settles at his paternal aunt's husband's area after leaving home in order to try and raise a family. MaNdlovu has a baby girl Siphiwe, who thrives, and Mloyiswa only goes back home to check on his father who is neglected and to see how his home is since his family has been away for a long time. His resentment of his mother is reinforced by the discovery that she has been using the church as a cover for her witchcraft activities. It is implied that the death of Mloyiswa and MaNdlovu's children was attributable to MaSibanda since she was proved a witch whilst Siphiwe thrived because she had been away from the home where MaSibanda stayed. Thus the source of conflict between Mloyiswa and his mother was partly the death of his children and partly the neglect of his father and the unreasonable behaviour of his mother.

In *Kutheni* by Mthethwa, the relationship between Ntonga and MaMthombeni deteriorates when MaMthombeni discovers that Ntombi had faked pregnancy in order to get Ntonga to marry her. MaMthombeni tries to suggest to her son Ntonga that his wife was not being honest about her supposed pregnancy. Ntonga gets angry and accuses his mother of trying to separate him from his wife. He moves from home with his wife and they go to town, after the quarrel. Ntombi subsequently neglects Ntonga and feeds him a love portion that makes him stupid and sick.

Ntonga just manages to get himself home to his mother and father where he collapses and is seriously ill for some time. It turns out that Ntombi has been 'fixed' by an old woman who had since died, so that Ntombi could not conceive. Her guardian is called and her family tried and found guilty of cheating Ntonga's family by marrying off to them, with prior knowledge, a barren woman. Ntonga's family's cattle are returned and he marries another woman who has children. Thus his relationship with his family and mother is restored.

In Stella Mandebvu's *Ndochema Naani?*, the relationship between Mubayiwa and his mother has already been described. It is clear that Munhamo, the mother initially feared that Mubayiwa's wife might stand in the way of her son and herself. However, Mhurai turns out to be a dutiful and hardworking wife to Mubayiwa so that his mother finds no reason to resent and hate her. The conflict betwen Mubayiwa and his mother results from his father's death, Vimbai's suicide, Munhamo's relationship with Zimwai and its role in Vimbai's death.

In Giles Kuimba's *Rurimi Inyoka*, the conflict and tension between the mother of Simon and Simon results from the fact that Vida, Simon's wife does not bear a child, a year after marriage. Simon's mother tries to get Simon's brother George to sleep with Vida so that she can find out whether it is her son or Vida who is barren. To Simon, she suggests that he should try other women so that she would know whether Simon could bear children or not. She hopes that Simon will impregnate his ex-girlfriend, Jane, thus leading to the breakup of Simon and Vida's marriage. Vida refuses to sleep with George. George is in turn scandalised and embarrassed by his mother's machinations. Simon refuses to sleep with Jane even when she visits him at his house one evening in Harare. Vida eventually gets pregnant and Simon's mother's plans are frustrated.

In Aaron Moyo's *Ziva Kwawakabva*, the mother-son relationship between VaTamai and Ngoni is strained on occasion because of VaTamai's belief in witchcraft and her very traditional outlook. She does not approve of the long years he spends at school and university given that she and her husband have to sell all their wealth to send and keep him at school. When he develops eye problems she insists that they consult a diviner and healer. The healer gives them charms and instructs them to get Ngoni to discard his spectacles. Ngoni wants to go to school and continue his education. His father Masvinyange supports this idea since he has a high regard for school education and the possibilities open to educated people. Ngoni finishes his 'A' levels but does not get a job. He refuses to do manual work in the farms and mines and remains unemployed for a year to the regret and disappointment of his parents. His mother's predictions and warnings seem to be borne out since Ngoni's education does not benefit them in any way. Ngoni is admitted to the university the following year and for three years he writes home very seldom. His mother is frustrated and misses him since he is the only child they have. After Ngoni graduates, the parents think their lives will improve. That does not happen because Ngoni marries a wife from a business family and forgets about his family who he considers to be uneducated and uncivilised. Rudo, Ngoni's wife, turns Ngoni's parents out of their house in Harare and they go back home dispirited and heartbroken. Ngoni's mother reminds her husband that she had always been against sending Ngoni to school. She indicates that it is her husband's fault that Ngoni is behaving so callously since Masvinyange, the husband, was the one who championed Ngoni's desire for schooling. Ngoni is taken ill and all the Western doctors in Harare cannot cure him. Eventually, Rudo brings him to his parents and leaves him there. They call the diviner and healer who nurses him back to health. This experience gets Ngoni to reconsider his attitude and relationship to his parents. He builds them a house and realises the errors of his ways. He is reconciled to his parents. His mother is happy since she can now point out her son to her neighbours who used to chide her and her husband for wasting their money sending Ngoni to school. However, even while all this is taking place, Ngoni's mother is loath to put the blame completely on her son. She sometimes thinks and says that Rudo, the witch, as she had described her in a letter to Ngoni, had influenced Ngoni against his parents. She is alternately condemning and condoning when it comes to her judgement of Ngoni. She has a soft spot for him despite all the mistreatment that has been meted out to her and her husband by Ngoni.

The relationship between mothers and married sons tends to be antagonistic especially if the son sides with his wife on various issues. In all the novels and examples quoted above, there is no instance where the mother did not try to harm the son's wife or her children by words or deed. Only in the case Munhamo, Mubayiwa's mother and his wife Mhurai, did them other of the husband actually like the wife of her son to the extent that she did not say or do nasty things to her after she had married the son. It has already been stated in Munhamo and Mhurai's case that before Mubayiwa married Mhurai, Munhamo was very apprehensive and has even told her children that Mhurai's grandmother was a witch.

As mothers-in-law, women who are elderly are invariably portrayed as malevolent towards their daughters-in-law and ultimately to their married sons. Their malevolence may be a result of the daughter-in-law's inability to have children, the son's neglect of his parents after marriage, competition with the daughter-in-law over the disposal of the son's income or jealousy for the son's affection and attention. These phenomena are interesting in that fathers-in-law of women as fathers of married sons, are very seldom portrayed as unreasonable, demanding or cruel. Most of them are very good to their daughters-in-law and yet the father's of sons are the ones who have the right to expect more from women marrying into their patrilineage. When women marry into their husband's patrilineages they are not full 'executive' members of that patrilineage as the women themselves say, are made to say, or are told in the novels and stories. The mothers-in-law, however, are seen by writers as powerful even in such situations.

In *Kutheni* by Mthethwa, MaMthombeni actually tells her son Ntonga that the Mhlanga clan will not waste their cattle paying for a barren woman, a dog and prostitute who came to cause trouble between her family and their neighbours. Simon's mother in Kuimba's *Rurimi Inyoka*, hangs on to the diviner's word that is is Vida's ex-boyfriend who has 'tied' her so that she cannot have a child. Vida's grandmother who is dead had supposedly let that happen to get Vida to accept the witchcraft she wanted Vida to inherit. Vida is supposed to have refused this. Simon's mother feels that Simon had wasted his cattle on a wife who is barren. Simon's mother tries to get Vida to fall pregnant by George, Simon's brother. This is unheard of traditionally since it was the duty of the men and women in a man's lineage to try to make this very delicate arrangement with their brother or brother's son if the latter was barren. A mother did not talk to her sons about sex or any affairs of the sleeping mat since she was not in the category of confidantes of a man on sexual matters. Even George is scandalised by his mother's suggestion.

Sons, on the other hand, also seem at best inept and at worst ineffectual when it comes to managing the relationships between their wives and mothers. After consulting, the diviner, Simon picks a quarrel with Vida over the issue of the ex-boyfriend. They make up the quarrel but Vida has to live with Simon's mother and her attempts to break up Simon and Vida's marriage. Simon reassures Vida that he loves her and that they would have children eventually but he does not realise what a bad time Vida is going through with his mother, the neighbours and Jane. In fact, Simon fails to 'read' his mother's plans and to recognise why she wants Vida to remain behind in the country or why Jane is coming to Harare. He is insensitive to his wife's feelings and emotional state.

Simon's sister, Mai Musindo, goes as far as accusing Vida of adultery and this results in VaTigere, Simon's father sending Vida to Simon and thrashing Mai Musindo and sending her back to her marital home. Simon remains ignorant of all this because his wife and father agree not to tell him. Simon actually fails to realise how far Jane and his mother are willing to go in trying to break up his marriage. He has never spoken strongly in support of his wife except to Vida herself. His mother takes so many liberties in her behaviour to Vida because she realises that she can exploit Simon's lack of perception. In contrast to Simon, his father knows his wife's capabilities and restrains her strongly when he can.

In *Ziva Kwawakabva*, by Aaron Moyo, Ngoni fails to moderate between his wife and his mother. He does not act to restrain Rudo from behaving badly to his parents but neither does he try to get his mother to understand that Rudo, his wife, has a waged job and thus cannot go to the communal lands to help her to plough their fields. This results in Rudo looking down on and mistreating his parents while his mother calls Rudo a witch, as VaTamai believes she has been told this by a diviner in Chirimanzu. The women then hate and abuse each other while Ngoni stands helpless and ineffectual between them, and by default, his wife gains the upper hand most of the time.

In Mungoshi's story 'The Victim' Mangazva is totally cowed by his mother and he even collaborates with her in undermining his wife. In his case, he is not only indifferent to his wife but he actively insults or scolds her while kowtowing to his mother. This gives his mother the ability to tell off his wife without fear of reprimand from him.

In a few instances, the sons do stand up for their wives against the mothers-in-law. Ntonga in *Kutheni* defends his wife against his mother but then, in the end, it turns out that the wife had been deceitful and had harmed her husband with portions calculated to stupefy him. Thus the sons tend to remain uninvolved or to refuse to commit themselves actively either way. They may react by moving home, counselling their wives to be silent, or leave the situations to resolve itself. Rarely do they take a stance against their mothers as Ntonga did.

There are some possible explanations for this reaction to mothers by sons. There is the fact that mothers will ultimately accept their children back no matter how grievously they have harmed their parents. The ties that bind mothers and children are strong. A good example of this is Ngoni's mother in *Ziva Kwawakabva*. Ngoni's mother is the first to forgive and accept him after Rudo dumps him at his parent's home. Despite the fact that she was the first to condemn his behaviour and villify his wife, she is also more willing than his father to forgive him. The same applies to MaMthombeni, Ntonga's mother after Ntanga gets seriously ill and comes home. It is also very important to recognise the fact that Shona and Ndebele societies are patrilineal, therefore the security of mothers in marriage rests with their sons. Sons are important in competition against the claims of co-wives' sons and for the husbands' affection. Without sons, women's positions are risky in their husband's lineages since sons can inherit wealth while daughters cannot do so. Thus sons have a better chance of maintaining their mothers materially in cases of widowhood, divorce, etc. Daughters marry into other patrilineages and cannot customarily take their parents with them. Thus married sons have a stake in keeping both mothers and wives unalienated because wives provide the routine day to day sustenance such as food, clean houses, clothes and bearing children while mothers champion the causes of those sons with the husbands and fathers and against the claims of other sons of co-wives in polygamous marriages. Thus the ambivalent stance of sons towards mothers and wives intensifies the conflict between wives and mothers to the detriment of both. It precludes the development of strong relationships between wives and mothers while leaving the possibility of relating to both open to the son-husband. At the same time, both women are not of the son-husband's patrilineage and have some common interests which they cannot realise because of their relation to the man. Thus this conflict highlights the relative dependence of married women either as mothers or as wives. Both depend on sons and husbands for mediating and securing their positions in marriage. The conflict also highlights the differences in power within the family between older and younger women. Older women with grown up, married sons have greater powers in their married home than the younger women with very young or no children.

In contrast to mothers-in-law and the intercalary position in the lineages of their husbands, fathers-in-law are portrayed as very pleasant and likeable figures. The unreasonable ones are few and far between. In Mungoshi's *Kunyarara Hakusi Kutaura?* Ruth tells of her husband's father's attempt to rape her. Her husband Mazarura sometimes acts as if he does not believe that the incident actually took place. In fact it is fathers and mothers of women who often have negative images. In *Ngitshilo Ngitshilo* by M. Ngwenya it is Mabhena, Nhlokotshiyane's father who is unreasonable because he wants to choose a husband who is uneducated for his daughter who is a State Registered Nurse. In Masiye's *Wangithengisela Umntanakhe*, it is Mlalazi, Ntombiyezwe's father who charges Ndlalambi an exhorbitant sum of money as *lobolo* (bride wealth). Even then, the mothers of women are depicted as far more unreasonable than their fathers as we shall see when the relationship of mothers and daughters is examined. Fathers of men are generally depicted in a sympathetic light as for example, Simon's father in Kuimba's *Rurimi Inyoka*, Masvinyange Ngoni's father in *Ziva Kwawakabva*, Rwandibva's father Shoperai in Sharai Mukonoweshuro's *Ndakakutadzirei*, Mubayiwa's father VaZindoga in Mandebvu's *Ndochema Naani*, Thembeni's father Mdlongwa in Khiyaza's *Ngiphilelani*, MaMpofu's father Mpofu in *Akulazulu Emhlabeni*, Mloyiswa's father Nyathi in *Umzenzi Kakhalelwa*. Mangazva's father in Mungoshi's story 'The Victim' and Kute's fatehr in *Some Kinds of Wounds*. In general, the parents of women tend to be negatively characterised and when it comes to the parents of men it is the mothers who are more negatively portrayed than the fathers.

This phenomenon and imagery can be explained on different levels. On one hand, older men and heads of patrilineages are most powerful and influential in formal, public, family and lineage politics. Institutionally they have power which has a material base in cattle, land use rights and control over labour in the lineage. Their power is secure and legitimate. Their wives' power is more informal and is mediated through the husbands. For that reason the mothers of men have to resort to manipulation and informal influence. This is reflected by their insecurity and attempts to control son's lives which are a source of security. By the same token, the patrilineages of women are the wife-givers in marriage and their daughters' lack of formal institutional power and security in marriage puts them at a disadvantage *vis-a-vis* the groom's patrilineage. This explains partly, the higher incidence of unreasonable parents of women in general, and fathers in particular. Fathers try to marry off daughters under the most advantageous material arrangements they can get away with. This is examplified by Mlalazi's demand on his son-in-law, Ndlalambi, in *Wangithengisela Umntanakhe*. At another level, fathers of women may try to assert their dominance on daughters while ameliorating their daughters' potential formal power disadvantage in a married home by insisting that daughters' should marry people known to the parents, preferably neighbours. This is illustrated by Mabhena's attempt to get Nhlokotshiyane married to Mayihlome, who is the son of his neighbour Zibunuzempi. This was an attempt by Mabhena to get a husband for his daughter, a husband who would recognise and be suitably impressed by the status of a father-in-law he knew. This would also ensure to some extent, Nhlokotshiyane's status and respect in her marital home. A husband who was a stranger would not be as impressed or as socially bound by neighbourly ties and expectations when it came to the regard and status he and his family accorded to a wife.

The same can be said of Nomalanga's father, Jola, when he refused to let Jojo Ncube marry Nomalanga on the grounds that Ncube was not a Fengu in N.M. Ncube's *Ukungazi Kufana Lokufa*. Thus mothers of sons and daughters are generally possessive of their children particularly sons because of the advantages and security sons are supposed to assure their mothers. However, parents of women are generally depicted as more calculating and difficult especially when the daughters are to be married. This is partly because they are trying to get maximum advantage from the marriage of their daughter who will be transferred to a different lineage where she will not have the same formal power as the women of her affinal lineage. The other reason is that the parents recognise her relative disadvantage especially if she is marrying strangers thus they may try to discourage her or make it difficult for the marriage to take place at all.

Mothers and daughters

The relationship between mothers and daughters is more intense and less fraught with tension than that of mothers and sons in Zimbabwean literature. This applies regardless of the class and marital status of the mothers and the daughters. It is only rarely that there is overt tension and long-standing antagonism between mothers and daughters. Only when there is a stepmother is the relationship between stepmother and stepdaughter intensely antagonistic.

In Nyamfukudza's story 'Lucia', the reader gets the feeling that Lucia's tragedy is that her mother is not present. She had to handle the burden of womanhood without her 'real mother' and this is why womanhood turns out to be such a tragedy for her. In Mungoshi's story, 'The Flood', Mhondiwa's wife is depicted as masterful over her husband who is afraid of her. The wife's mother is said to have been a witch who always got what she wanted. The daughter is said to have inherited her mother's witching streak. The reader gets the impression that mother and daughter were very close and had similar characters and interests. From Giles Kuimba's *Rurimi Inyoka*, Vida and her mother's relationship is close and loving. Vida's mother comes to meet her daughter secretly in Harare in order to try to solve her daughter's problem of childlessness. In the same novel, Simon's mother and her daughter Mai Musindo are close and united especially against Vida whom they try to get rid of. They plot together to discomfit Vida during Simon's absence. In *Ziva Kwawakabva* MaKhumalo and her daughter Rudo get on very well and MaKhumalo inculcates her values in her daughter. She tries to aid Rudo when Ngoni gets ill. In Chakaipa's *Garandichauya*, the reader is shown a good example of mother-daughter solidarity. Muchaneta and her mother are agreed in terms of what Muchaneta must do to seduce men for material benefit. In *Pafunge* by Tsodzo, Rudo Moyo's tragedy, like Lucia's, is that her mother had died and she has nobody to look after her and help her avert the tragedies that can accompany womanhood. In *Sara Ugarike* by N. Hamandishe, Marujata's mother VaMaidei, colludes in her daughter's affair with Kurimahufamba even though Marujata has not completed the one year's celibacy period expected of a widow. Actually VaMaidei gives her daughter poison to get rid of Marujata's husband, Mukomondera.

In *Akulazulu Emhlabeni* by N.S. Sigogo, MaMpofu's mother MaNkala is also characterised as fiercely partisan and supportive of her daughter even before she knows the facts about the circumstances in which her daughter left her husband. In *Wangithengisela Umtanakhe*, Ntombi's mother actually encourages her to go to her husband against her father's will even in the face of the threat that Ntombi's mother would also be kicked out with her daughter by the husband if Ntombi left. Ntombi leaves and her mother leaves to stay at her husband's elder brother's home. In *Kutheni*, Sinikiwe, Ntonga's sister is in accord with her mother in the view that

Ntonga is led by his wife by the nose and that Ntombi should go since she could not bear children. At the same time Ntombi's mother is very supportive of her daughter who has appealed to her for help over her problem in bearing a child. Mabhena, Ntombi's mother sends Ntombi some medicine for drinking, putting in her husband's food, bathing and inhaling. In fact the norm is for mothers and daughters to get on very well.

MaSibanda and her daughter Deliwe are very close. Deliwe is the helper to her mother and she has to be cleansed when it is discovered that she was the inheritor of her mother's witchcraft. It is implied that Deliwe was on apprentice to her mother's 'profession' because she was the closest to her.

There are very few and rare instances when mothers and daughters do not see eye to eye. In *Ngitshilo Ngitshilo*, Nhlokotshiyane's mother Madebe is too scared to intervene on her daughter's behalf to try to persuade her father to let her marry a man of her choice. Instead, Madebe shares her husband's bigotry and tribalistic view of Nhlokotshiyane's boyfriend whom Nhlokotshiyane loves. She does not want Nhlokotshiyane to marry a *hole* i.e. a person of Shona extraction incorporated into the Ndebele state in pre-colonial Zimbabwe.

In Mungoshi's *Makunun'unu Maodzamwoyo*, Monica and Tendai do not get on with their mother VaChingweru who tries to marry off Monica to an old man. Monica is raped by Mujubheki the man chosen for her by her mother but she manages to procure herself an abortion. VaChingweru poisons Timoti, Monica's boyfriend. She is a nasty grandmother to Tendai's children and calls Tendai a prostitute because Tendai is living alone after her divorce from her husband.

It is important to note that male writers stress the collusion between mothers and their daughters whilst female writers do not necessarily give the relationship overwhelming prominence. This can be explained by the fact that husbands perceive their mothers-in-law as having more influence than them over their wives' lives. Women may take a close relationship with their mothers for granted and are given so much that they are not struck by it. Men tend to see this relationship as negative in a lot of instances where mothers misguide married daughters, giving them harmful portions to feed their husbands and encouraging them to stand up to their husbands in arguments. However, it is important to realise that mothers rear children till they marry and for women, advice about how to handle a household, children and a husband is most available from a mother who is the most experienced and closest person to women. Like her mother, a married daughter has moved out of her own patrilineage and is learning how to cope in a new and alien environment. Mother-daughter relationships tend to be manipulative, informal and exclusive of men hence their threat to men. Both women teach and learn about how to manoeuvre as mothers and married women and this explains the view by sons, brothers, fathers and husbands that sisters, mothers and daughters misguide each other and collude over family issues.

As daughters, women also have brothers and there is a dependency relationship between women and their brothers. In youth, there is usually no tension between women and their brothers but after brothers' marriage, tension may arise when sisters ally themselves with mothers against brothers' wives.

So far this chapter has dealt with women's images as mothers. However, it is necessary to consider the image of women as stepmothers too. In all the novels and stories examined, there is no instance where the stepmother is portrayed positively. In fact, Lucia, *Ngiphilelani* by G. Khiyaza and *Ndakakutadzirei* by Mukonoweshuro all have negative images of stepmothers especially towards female stepchildren. Female stepchildren spend their time doing women's work in the fields and household hence they feel the authority and maltreatment by the stepmother more directly. A stepmother may resent the children of the wife who is divorced or dead because these children may have prior claims on their fathers' wealth particularly if they are boys. The stepmother may view the stepchildren as competition for her and her children over the affection of the husband. It could also be that the main reason why the stepmother was married was to look after the first or former wife's children and the stepmother may resent this.

Most writers take the view that the stepmother has so much influence over the husband that he is blinded to her cruelty to his children.

This chapter has explored and outlined the dominant images of women as mothers in the literature of Zimbabwe by black writers. Variations have been noted in the images of mothers that young and married sons hold. Tensions and compatibilities between mothers and sons have been outlined. While examining how mothers and sons relate to each other, it was also necessary to indicate the way mothers relate to their sons' wives. Very often, the latter relationship was observed to be fraught with tension and intrigue although and in spite of the fact that both categories of women are not members of affinal patrilineages. Their attempts to strengthen their positions in their affinal homes partly explain the tension. In part the attempts by mothers to retain control over their sons and the attempts by wives to assert control over husbands put mothers-in-law against their daughters-in-law.

With regard to women and daughters, the relationship is more harmonious and rarely do they clash. It is only when mothers try to decide on and direct their daughters' lives too tightly and when daughters get to resent their mothers' control that conflict results. When daughters perceive mothers to be using them for their own ends, daughters may revolt. Thus, on the whole, daughters tend to view their mothers in a very positive light.

Stepmothers are not viewed positively except by their own children. The stepmothers are resented and viewed as interlopers who are cruel and destructive towards the stepchildren. The husbands of the women who are stepmothers may not have this view all the time but they too seem to be on guard and they seem to expect some degree of disregard of their former wives' children by the new wives. Stepmothers usually fail in their designs against stepchildren and their own children usually do not turn out well because they are spoilt and inconsiderate even of their mothers. This makes the stepmothers realise the errors of their ways, and revise their perception and treatment of their stepchildren.

Notes to Chapter 1 Women as mothers

1. page 25, *Aftermaths*, The College Press, 1983
2. page 28, *ibid*
3. page 26, *Some Kinds of Wounds*, Mambo Press, 1980
4. page 15, *Kutheni*, The College Press, 1982
5. page 127. *Some Kinds of Wounds*, Mambo Press, 1980

2

Women as wives

The ideal wife

Different authors tend to depict the images of wives in varying ways. Most authors let their characters comment on what constitutes an ideal wife. In some cases, the authors of novels or short stories will editorialise about the characters they are writing.

The role of wife is closely tied to that of the husband and children. A wife is judged in terms of how she behaves towards her husband and how she looks after him, the household and the children. The ideal wife is one who is totally committed to serving the interests of her husband and her children even at the risk of martyring or sacrificing her own interests. The most obvious example of an idela wife is Tsitsi (Mercy) in Chakaipa's *Garandichauya*. Tsitsi is the best example of an ideal wife for several reasons. She abandons her education to marry Matamba. She is a virgin when she marries him and this is acknowledged by her husband's family. Tsitsi has a son appropriately named Nhamoinesu (Trouble is with us) because the child's father was behaving badly towards the mother. Matamba goes to gown (Gatooma) and stays away for two years without ever visiting his wife. Tsitsi waits patiently during those two years till she decides to go to look for him in town. She finds him living with Muchaneta, another woman. When Matamba arrives from work he finds Tsitsi there. He disowns her as his wife and asserts that his only wife is Muchaneta. He says Tsitsi is only an old girlfriend. A fight between Tsitsi and Muchaneta ensues and Matamba intervenes in Muchaneta's favour. Tsitsi is told by Matamba to go back to the country and wait for his return. Tsitsi leaves and goes back to her home and lives a celibate life, turning away suitors who are interested in marrying her. Her aunt reinforces her stance by telling her that in their paternal clan no woman cooks for two husbands while the first husband is still alive implying that no woman in their clan remarries unless she has been widowed. Tsisti's behaviour is constrasted with that of Handisumbe's wife who has remarried after being chased away by Handisumbe when he was having an affair with Muchaneta. Handisumbe proposes marriage to Tsitsi but she turns him down and waits for Matamba.

It is only when Matamba is destitute and blind after a beating set up by Muchaneta that a kindly teacher takes him back to his wife, Tsitsi. Tsitsi says she is happy to take him, the father of her children, back. She says that her shame is erased since her children now have a father. She says he did not do much that was wrong, that all that counts is the fact that he is alive. She says it does not matter that Matamba is blind, he is *her* blind husband and she cannot turn away the father of her children simply because he is blind. She is willing to forget all the wrong he did her.

Another ideal wife is Vida in *Rurimi Inyoka*. Despite all the taunting, provocation and general maltreatment by her mother-in-law and neighbours, she endures and sticks with her husband. When Simon gets jealous about Vida's ex-boyfriend, he alludes to the diviner's statement that it is because of this ex-boyfriend's spell that she cannot conceive and bear a child. Vida is all sweetness even then and reasons with him about all the possible causes of childlessness in a couple. She then reassures him of her love and offers to go to a medical doctor for examination and tests on the understanding that she will give him a divorce if it is discovered that they cannot have a child. She however, offers to stay with him regardless if it is found that he cannot have children. She reminds him that she promised, in her wedding vows, that she would stay with him in sickness and in health, poverty or wealth, sadness or happiness till death parted them and she aimed to keep that promise. These words melt Simon's heart and he regrets his unreasonable jealousy that had made him accuse her of infertility because of her ex-boyfriend. Vida eventually fulfills the requirement for qualifying as an ideal wife by getting pregnant.

Mhurai, Mubayiwa's wife is also depicted, in *Ndochema Naani?*, as an ideal wife. She is hardworking and bears her husband a son. In *Ndakakutadzirei* Shongedzai waits faithfully for her husband, Rwandibva, who has gone to study in America. She is ill-treated by her husband's stepmother and stepsister. She does not complain or quarrel with them. When Rwandibva believes the false story that Shongedzai had an affair when he had gone to visit his father's home, he calls her a prostitute, beats her up and breaks her arm. Shongedzai covers up for her husband by lying to her parents that she fell and broke her arm. This is after her husband had discovered that the man purpoted to be her lover was a male relative, VaTorega. She still insists that her husband is good, that it is his relatives who are difficult. She does not hold him responsible for believing unsubstantiated rumours about his wife. Rwandibva subsequently regrets having misjudged his wife and asks for her forgiveness. She forgives him and goes back to their home.

In *Sara Ugarike*, Ndaizivei, Kurimahufamba's wife is an example of an ideal wife. She sees her husband conduct his affair with Marujata. When she complains, her mother-in-law VaMarwei counsels her to persevere and not to worry as long as Kurima conducts his affairs outside the home. She is told by VaMarwei that all marriages are like that and that men behave that way and that if she ignored Kurima's bad behaviour, he would get tired an behave himself. VaMarwei tells Ndaizivei not to contemplate leaving her son to be raised without her. Marwei says after all, all things come to an end and bad times usually precede good ones, if Ndaizivei weathers these problems, she would tell them as stories to her children.

Ndaizivei takes this advice and the result is that Kurima brings Marujata to stay as second wife. Kurima lands in jail and this causes problems for Ndaizivei. In the end, she is widowed after suffering the indignity of constant quarrels with Marujata and embarrassment at having a criminal for a husband. She still has to start fending for herself and her son from scratch or depend on his parents until she remarries or dies.

In *Ngitshilo Ngitshilo*, Madebe, Nhlokotshiyane's mother is ideal as a wife in the sense that she agrees with her husband's sentiments over the choice of a husband for their daughter. She sides with her husband against her daughter. It must be borne in mind that Nhlokotshiyane was the favourite child of her father. Her mother Madebe was the second of three wives of Mabhena and she would prejudice her own and her daughter's position by allowing her daughter to have her way against the father. Madebe also shared her husband's views on the undesirability of marrying *holes* i.e. people of Shona extraction who were incorporated into the Ndebele state in pre-colonial Zimbabwe whom she and her husband regard as inferior.

In *Umzenzi Kakhalelwa*, MaNdlovu is the ideal wife to Mloyiswa Nyathi. She stoically bears the death of her children in infancy while staying at her husband's home. She is hardworking and eager to keep the peace between her husband and mother-in-law.

Thus the women who are idealised may be those women who are obedient to their husbands even if the husbands are wrong and unreasonable. They are women who do not complain when they are badly treated. They patiently wait for their husbands to recognise their virtue and they may actually shield their husbands from the consequences of unreasonable or cruel behaviour.

A more detailed analysis of the motivation underlying these ideal wives' actions is necessary in order to understand why they act as they do and are portrayed as they are. The stories and novels cited here were written between 1963 and 1983. All of these years save the last three straddle the colonial period in Zimbabwe. During that time, the economy of Zimbabwe had evolved into a capitalist one and it built on the patriarchy that could facilitate the development of capitalism also got strengthened within the family, the economy, and the polity. This was manifested by more emphasis on the rights of males to waged jobs, to school education, to jural power in the family. During the colonial era, most women remained outside the formal school system, the polity and their encounter with capitalism was mediated throught their husbands in waged jobs. To keep the family structure functional to subsistence and recompositon of black labour, rights to land for women could only be mediated through their patrilineages or through husbands who were labour migrants and absent from home most of the time. This structural arrangement of the society and economy increased women's dependence on men for access to land, and to education since fees needed to be paid in cash. It also had the effect of discouraging the education of women and their access to waged jobs. The only alternative for women was to till the land as wives in the subsistence sector of the economy. For such land, women depended on men as husbands, fathers or guardians. Thus any woman who had any intelligence realised that for most of her adult life, her husband was the most important person in terms of securing her access to land from which to earn a living. She could not afford to alienate her husband's affections since this would threaten her means of earning or producing a living. Women without any resources to earn a living in the society except land had no choice but be obedient to their husbands. These women are ideals through force of circumstances and absence of real choices rather than through their own wishes.

This 'ideal' state of these women tends to be cheapened and diminished by the fact that they do not choose it. It is socially difficult for them to be otherwise and this calls into question whatever virtue one may have seen in their behaviour. In fact, it is a matter of making a virtue out of necessity since they had no other real choices.

A more detailed examination of one such ideal wife is useful in illustrating the problems involved in such portrayals of 'ideals'. Chakaipa characterised Tsitsi as the most admirable, morally beautiful character in *Garandichauya*. Tsitsi sacrifices her education to marry Matamba. She is neglected, beaten and disowned by her husband and then she has to look after him when he is destitute and blind. Tsitsi is idealised because she agrees to look after her husband after he has rendered himself helpless and unproductive around the home. He spends the best and most productive years of his life looking after other women except his wife and children. Tsisti is seen as morally virtuous because she conforms to the image of the 'ideal' wife who obeys her husband's orders even while he is being cruel to her. This is more like masochism then virtue! As Kahari (1972) observes, the author does not bother to elaborate on Tsitsi's character. We never get an idea of all the processes and challenges that are involved in the quest for virtue. We only see Tsitsi when she is married, chased away by her husband and when she is accepting him back. On one level, her goodness and wisdom can be questioned in terms of her marrying a man who is spoilt as a son already. She does not recognise this fact. Secondly, she is disowned by her husband but continues to deny herself the company of other men by refusing to remarry. One cannot help but be disgruntled with her self-righteousness and reason for turning down other suitors, namely that her husband is still alive. In fact she does not know whether he is dead or alive so her reasoning is questionable. Thirdly, her self-righteous acceptance of Matamba when he comes home blind and penitent is exasperating. If at least she had shown some doubts, resentment or reluctance before finally taking him back, one would have identified with her as a human being with feelings that could be hurt, and a capacity to feel injured and slighted. Tsitsi's goodness is cloying particularly to a female reader. She is self-denying to the point of absurdity.

On another level, it must be recognised that Tsitsi is the creation of Chakaipa who may not be sensitive to the way a woman may view the reaction of Tsitsi to Matemba's exploits. In fact is it more revealing to analyse Tsitsi's reason for taking back Matamba. These reasons may not be interpreted as nobly as Chakaipa may have intended them to be. Tsitsi states that she is happy because the father of her children is back. She says she had been ashamed because her children had no father. This view is very illuminating of both Tsitsi and her creator, Chakaipa. She is happy for her children since they now have a socially and physically present and recognisable father. For her children, the figurehead of a father is important despite the fact that he has not supported them materially and is not likely to do so to any great extent as an unskilled and barely educated blind man. Matamba's presence also makes Tsitsi respectable. A divorced or single mother did not have a high status or the wherewithal to make a good material living. She was viewed as a failure since she had not succeeded in keeping her husband or getting one. She was a threat to existing marriages since she could consort with the husbands of other women. The presence of a husband, albeit a dependent, disabled one was preferable to having no husband at all for a woman in Tsitsi's situation. Matamba's presence reinstated Tsitsi's self esteem and respectability. At no point does Tsitsi express joy because *her husband* is back. Tsitsi goes on to say that Matamba did not do much that was wrong, what counts most is that he is alive. This is a telling statement since the reader knows that Matamba did do much that was wrong in neglecting his children and treating his wife brutally. One feels reluctant and unable to agree with Tsitsi's statement since she is either being polite, kind and diplomatic for a reason or is just incapable of evaluating the behaviour of others around her. In fact Matamba himself states that he has treated her badly and that he wishes to die if only to express how grievously he has mistreated her. Tsitsi goes on to say that blindness does not matter, he is *her* blind husband and she cannot turn away her children's father because he is blind. He may have erred but she is willing to forget all the wrongs he did her.

Tsitsi's reiteration that Matamba is the father of her children does point to the fact that Tsitsi's posture is pragmatic and not merely an expression of her innate or inculcated virtue. Kahari (1972) holds that Matamba never really loved Tsitsi and their relationship continues in the absence of Matamba because of custom which forecloses many alternative options to Tsitsi. In fact, Tsitsi's acceptance of Matamba may be pragmatic and self interested in that it is calcualted to help her preserve a good social position as a known and present man's wife, avoid any social scandal that might accompany a woman of divorced or deserted status while also safeguarding her children's interests. In Shona society, power and influence for women comes about through age, marriage and motherhood. Thus marriage is the only realistic option open to unskilled, uneducated rural women who want social acceptability. Matamba's presence and Tsitsi's status as a wife helps Tsitsi regain control especially given that her husband is blind. If he had not been blind, she could possibly have lost some of the power she had gained as the rearer of her children and the provider for all their needs. In the end Tsitsi is more powerful because she does not rely on a husband for her livelihood on a day to day basis although she may realise her rights to land use through his patrilineage.

It is also noteworthy that it is the 'ideal' wives who are most brutalised and maltreated without cause. Vida in *Rurimi Inyoka* is harassed and humiliated by her mother-in-law, Simon's ex-girlfriend, Jane, Simon's sister Mai Musindo, Mai Zipfende and Mai Mashumba. Mhurai does not suffer a great deal except that her grandmother is accused of being a witch by Mubayiwa's mother. Shongedzai in *Ndakakutadzirei* is humiliated and harassed by her husband's stepsister and stepmother. She is called a prostitute and assaulted seriously by her husband. She breaks off her plans to continue her education after marriage. Madebe in *Ngitshilo Ngitshilo* is separated and alienated from her daughter when the latter refuses to marry the man of her father's choice. Madebe's co-wives glory in her troubles and they are not supportive of her. Madebe suffers when her husband considers her daughter as dead because of her disobedience to her father. In *Umzenzi Kakhalelwa*, MaNdlovu bravely bears the death of her infant children in suspicious circumstances at her husband's home. She remains the dutiful daughter-in-law until her husband takes her away. At least in MaNdlovu's case, she is not mistreated by her husband.

In the final analysis, one questions whether it is worth the heartache, suffering and brutalisation in order to approximate the ideal of a good wife. One gets the impression that it is very difficult to opt out of being an obedient wife given the material dependence of wives on husbands while it is just as difficult, if not more so, to try to be other than a 'good' wife. Those wives who remain obedient and self-sacrificing out of necessity have to continue to depend on the whims and mercies of those to whom they owe obedience and for whom they deny themselves. At the same time, if the sacrifice is refused or disregarded, then the ideal wives will be bereft and will have to look for other people for whom they can sacrifice or deny themselves.

The problem wives

Images of problem wives abound in Zimbabwean literature. There are many types of reasons to explain the problematic nature of these wives. These wives are 'problem' to the husbands in the novels and stories under consideration and to the novelists who may also be husbands themselves or may take a particular view about how 'proper' wives should behave. In Makhalisa's story 'Baby-snatcher', Ntombi the wife of Lizwe gets involved in the illegal adoption of a baby in an attempt to become an ideal wife by giving her husband a child. What is embarrassing is the fact that Ntombi firmly believes that she is the one who is not able to have a child when in fact it is her husband who cannot. Ntombi's situation is complex because she is trying to achieve the state of an ideal wife and she thinks she can succeed by adopting a child while her husband is away on a long course. She is going to tell him the child is his when he returns. What is galling though, is Lizwe's letter in which he confesses that the 'fault' is his but states that he would have divorced her if it was another man's child in spite of the fact that he has hidden the truth from her. Ntombi gets arrested before Lizwe's return and the whole affair is embarrassing to her family as well as Lizwe's. The problem with Ntombi is that she is so willing to assume the mantle of a martyr, victim as well as a failure who could not give her husband a child. Ntombi's attitude towards herself leads her to commit a criminal act. She is, however, saved by her husband's love and acceptance of her despite her act.

Ntombi is an ideal wife in the sense that she knows what was expected of her as a wife and tries to fulfil that expectation. She learns the hard way that in an attempt to approximate the ideal, one can hurt and embarrass oneself as well as loved ones around them. At the same time, the attempt may actually hinder the development of honesty between spouses. While Ntombi is trying so hard for a child, Lizwe does not feel courageous enough or bound to tell Ntombi the truth. Only when she has embarrassed herself and both their families, and in a disadvantaged position, does he feel it safe and necessary to tell her the truth. In the circumstances, he is able to bargain for her understanding in exchange for forgiving her. Only then does he feel he could offer her a second honeymoon and the choice to adopt any child she wants legally. He then tells her that his mother has left for the communal area only after Ntombi has gone through a harrowing time with Lizwe's mother who holds her responsible for their childlessness. It would have been more noble a gesture if he had got his mother to leave before Ntombi gets into trouble, not after, and all because Lizwe does not tell her that he suspects that he cannot father a baby.

Of the writers in English, Mungoshi's characterisation of wives in particular and women in general tends to be striking in one sense. Most of the women characters in his writing are very strong, large in life and domineering. In 'Who will stop the dark?', Zakeo's mother dwarfs her husband in word and deed. It is implied that she had something to do with her husband's weakness. The husband says 'A man's back is the man. Once his back is broken ... ' Zakeo's mother's eyes flash at that and silence the husband. The reader gets the impression that Zakeo's mother has indeed broken her husband's back. So cowed is the husband that even the small boy tries to protect his father from the grandfather and his mother's criticism. While Zakeo talks to his grandfather, there is a suggestion of a line of domineering women in Zakeo's father's life. Zakeo learns that his grandfather hates basket-weaving which is his dominated son's occupation. The old man informs Zakeo that it is Zakeo's grandmother, the old man's wife who taught Zakeo's father basket-weaving, a skill that the old man considers unmanly. So Zakeo's father's unmanning had been started by his mother and continued by his wife, Zakeo's mother. Thus the old man's wife and his son's wife had dominated and unmanned the old man's son. The old man tells Zakeo 'But your mother is your mother', while he thinks 'After all is said and done, basket-weaving never killed anyone. What kills is the rain and the hailstorms and the cold and the hunger when you are like this, when the echoes come'.[1] This is his way of telling Zakeo that mothers will get their way like his wife got her way with Zakeo's father by teaching him basket-weaving, part of the process of unmanning him. It seems as if he is resigned when he says that even when you are dominated by a wife or mother, you are not dead physically. What can kill you are the natural elements when you are hungry and unsheltered because of lack of that same wife or mother who dominates you.

Zakeo's mother snorts when the old man refers to his son, Zakeo's father. Zakeo will not even listen to his father as he should because the father has no authority in the home. Zakeo tells his grandfather how hurt he is by the taunts of other boys who refer to the fact that his father is dominated by his mother. 'They are always at me saying your father is your mother's horse ... '[2] Thus Zakeo's mother discomfits her son, her husband and father-in-law by the way she dominates her husband. She makes them all a laughing stock with the neighbours.

When Zakeo is getting stropped, his father tries to intervene and is stropped himself. We do get to hear the wife's feelings. She tells Zakeo that 'He never wanted your father to marry me'[3] referring to the old grandfather of Zakeo. This may explain why her relations with her husband and son are strained and the collusion of the grandfather in maintaining the strain. As a strong woman who recognises her husband's weakness, Zakeo's mother is isolated and lonely but she knows that she has to do the best for her son even if it is going to cost her the love of her son, husband and father-in-law. For the wife, the price of strength and determination is the denial of tenderness and approval by all those around her.

In 'The Victim', Mangazva's father is also dominated by his wife. He is introduced to the reader while sitting in his chair. 'He seemed to have taken a long time growing into his chair, so that he had become part of it like one of those strange parasite plants that one often sees growing from the branches of some very old trees. His shoulders were hunched, his head bent forward towards the fire as if he were listening to the stories the fire was telling him, stories of a much warmer distant country.'[4] The husband, Mangazva's father does not occupy the comfortable seat close to the fire. It is occupied by the wife, Mangazva's mother. The seat is cushioned for her comfort. She threatens to go and confront the family of Simba, who is supposed to have tried to kill her son. The husband, Mangazva's father is silent. When he finally interjects quickly to ask Mangazva not to involve Mr Moyo in the affair, the wife flares up and says 'But those people nearly killed your son and you sit there . . .'[5] Her statement is eloquent and expresses exactly what she thinks of her husband. When the husband tells Mangazva that his drinking, coming home late and inability to live with other people properly, his over dependence on his mother were the source and cause of Mangazva's problems, the wife, Mangazva's mother looks away at the wall. Then she spits 'Barking dogs and castrated bulls.'[6] That is telling on both her son and her husband. One cannot help feeling that she has crushed both her son and husband as the daughter-in-law suggests Mangazva's mother does to people.

In Mungoshi's story 'The day the bread van didn't come' we are treated to yet another castrating and domineering wife. Mrs Pfende is introduced to the reader as a verbally violent woman, barking orders to her husband who withdraws into himself from her violence. She speaks without looking at her husband and he, in turn, is afraid to ask her to repeat what she has said to him even though he has not heard clearly what she has said. Her husband looks at her furtively and hides behind his newspaper while he thinks 'Must be her time of month'. He is glad that he can think all these things without her hearing him. He considers this a way of getting back at her. Mr Pfende is mean and he shows this by selling a child an old, mouldy bun. His wife is disgusted by his action.

Mrs Pfende thinks excitedly about the bread delivery man. Mr Pfende has his suspicions and is jealous that her excitement is not for him. He could not give his wife any children and when he complains about the delivery man, calling him ' . . . a son of . . . ' she interrupts him with the words 'Better a son of a bitch than a father of nothing'. She continues 'Why don't you sell up and turn baker then, if you are that hot?'[8] then she laughs and muses 'I just wonder what kind of bread you would make—all doughy and watery, I suppose?'[9] She is obviously alluding to him sexually, suggesting impotence and lack of virility. She sits there brazenly knitting a jersey for the bread delivery man while he wonders whether she had heard all the things people said about him, namely, that he had sold his power to bear children for medicine to make him successful in business. He also feels that people's sympathies are with her since she had had her two boys with her deceased husband taken from her by the deceased husband's relatives. The relatives had accused her of being a witch as an explanation for the death of her husband. Since she is beautiful, the accusations are credible because people hold that beauty of that magnitude has to have a flaw somewhere. When Mrs Pfende learns that Moses the bread delivery man has died in a car accident, she starts propositioning the young man who has delivered the bread and the news about Moses. The young man flees and in anger, Mrs Pfende slaps her husband, breaks the glass and frame that holds their wedding photograph and tears up the photograph and marriage certificate. Mr Pfende only smiles in satisfaction because there are lots of people coming in to buy bread. He is not overly worried about the significance of the destroyed wedding photograph and marriage certificate as long as the money is pouring in.

In 'The Flood', also by Mungoshi, we encounter another man who is cuckolded and dominated by his wife. Mhondiwa has fought Chitauro over Mhondiwa's wife. Mhondiwa's wife is depicted as a bossy woman. She picks quarrels with him in public so that she can demonstrate to her friends how she handles a 'sleepy husband'. He is 'a bit afraid of her'[10] The wife has inherited and learned her ways from her own mother who had 'softened' her own husband with medicine to the extent that he became an idiot after which she killed him. This echoes the attiktude of Zakeo's grandfather in 'Who Will Stop the Dark?', who thought his son had been softened by his mother, then his wife.

Mhondiwa's wife does not leave him any food the day he is demoted from his position of boss-boy which is given to Chitauro. She compounds the insult by ' . . . hammering at how thirty-five Mhondiwa's were nothing to Chitauro's little finger'.[11] Mhondiwa gets angry and asks his wife whether she is having an affair with Chitauro. She asks 'O, my! Are you blind as well? I thought you knew. When you look at those children you call yours, do you tap your little tit telling yourself you did the job? Why don't you look at them and see if you could call any of them yours? Go ahead!'[12] She then calls her daughter Rumbidzai and asks her to show her father her nose and to tell him where she got it. Mhondiwa then beats his wife for the first time in their married life. He feels guilty about it though. The wife leaves and takes with her his lion skin belt that is his protector. He feels vulnerable without the belt. While Mhondiwa discusses women with other men, the old man Makiwa says women are men's death, that women destroy men despite the fact that men fool themselves into believing that they are the masters of their houses, that women do not recognise anything or anybody unless they own it or them. He continues on woman, 'She takes everything and leaves you as empty as a mealie husk after the harvest, as undefended as a snail without its shell, and finally, when you are completely broken and useless she sends you out to face the lion without a spear or a shield to defend yourself.'[13]

Mhondiwa thinks back on how he had been enjoined to look after his lion-skin belt by the medicine-man who had treated him during a serious illness when he was a child. He was asked not to tell his wife what it was for. He remembers how he had met his wife who had slept with him the night she met him. Three weeks later, she had told him she was expecting his baby and five months later, she had born a baby. She had given him an explanation that he did not understand but accepted all the same. The village people had laughed all the same. Mhondiwa had not understood why they laughed at him at the time. As old Makiwa says, '. . . you only realise too late that she has been sucking you since the day you saw her, lying, lying, lying, destroying and draining the blood out of you, draining the seed out of you, leaving you your empty name whose substances she has used, the empty husk she throws on the ash heap to rot.'[14] Mhondiwa gets so angry that he knifes Chitauro while they are drinking beer supposedly to reconcile their differences.

In Marechera's story, 'The House of Hunger,' the boy's mother cuckolds her husband in the same room she shares with her sons. She does not care that her sons know that she sleeps with other men or that they might tell their father about her. She humiliates her husband by beating him and throwing him out of the house one night when he and the boys come home drunk. She causes the neighbours to despise him because of her liaisons with other men.

While Marechera outlines the whorish and indecent behaviour of the mother and wife he does not glamourise or condone her drunken husband either. He shows the husband as a spinelss and violent man. The elder son also resembles his father in his violence towards the young woman who lives with him. The wife is strong and knows that she has to keep the family together even if it will cost her the respect of her sons. She is not in a position to afford respectability given her weak husband and the hostile racist, class society in which she rears her children. She cannot realise the ideal of the good and faithful wife. She has to choose whether to be an ideal wife with a broken family or a wife and mother who is not admired but protects her family albeit in an unrespectable fashion. Marechera is contemptuous of the wife, her sons, her husband and her neighbours. Nobody is spared. In the same story, the wife of the cook is known by the schoolboys to be cuckolding her husband with Jet, the assistant boarding master.

In Marechera's story 'The Writer's Grain', the wife of the teacher cuckolds her husband with a student and in 'Thought Tracks in the Snow', Rachel gets pregnant by another man who is not her husband.

In Nyamfukudza's story 'Guilt and Sorrow' the woman wonders about her lack of self-definition in her house since she is always there to fetch and carry for her husband. Her husband comes home and starts complaining about the problems he encounters at work each day. On this particular day she does not listen quietly but walks out of the room after telling him that he is only a small man, a messenger from Monday to Friday, so he should accept his lot or leave the job rather than moan every day. She feels wearied and downtrodden by marriage and poverty. 'No balls, that was his problem. Like her father and his mother,'[15] she thinks. Her father had been a weak character and it was her mother who had been responsible for keeping their family going. He had been a gentle person; ' . . . but it was all rather negative.'[16] He had exerted no authority in the home except when the children needed money or forms to be signed. Her father's mother was like his son, gentle and pious, constantly moaning and feeling sorry for herself. She thinks her grandmother could not have given her son, the woman's father, any strength or guts since the grandmother had none herself. This sentiment again echoes that of Zakeo's father who also saw mothers as unmanning, weakening or bequeathing weakness to their sons while strengthening their daughters by giving them advice, medicine and other mechanisms for dominating men in general and husbands and sons in particular.

The wife tells her husband that she has been thinking about taking a job, that there is one already waiting if she wants it. She tells him it is a two-hours a day job. He does not even bother to ask what job it is but laughs at the kind of pay he thinks she would get in a factory job of two hours a day. She does not tell him what the job is either but resents the fact that he shows no interest in it an all, preferring her to wait on him and listen to him moaning about his own job every day. When she starts her job at the studio, her husband is worried and anxious. He feels insecure since she also has her own job and no longer acts as his sounding board when he wants to moan and complain. She feels sad and lonely because he never thinks of comforting her or showing her much loving attention. She also feels sorry for herself because she has no children and is getting old.

The husband's attitude is not altogether negative however. She overhears him boasting about her job, saying he had not believed her and had thought she was seeing other men when she went out in the evening. She is so glad that she goes along covering up the lie her husband had told to a neighbour when the husband did not want to share a meal with the neighbour. The husband wins his bet against a neighbour who had doubted that it was the man's wife on the radio in the evening. 'Cunning bastard,' she thought, 'he would make money of of it, would he? But she was happy, a cloud had lifted from her heart.'[17]

In *Ziva Kwawakabva*, Ngoni's wife Rudo, dominates him thoroughly. She is from a wealthy family and behaves in a western way. She looks down on her husband's parents because they are poor and uneducated. She throws them out of her house because they are dirty and unkempt. She tells Ngoni's mother that her cracked feet would ruin her mats so the old woman has to stay out of the house. Ngoni is so influenced and dominated by Rudo's values that he does not invite his parents to his wedding. She influences Ngoni not to buy Shona records since she says they are a sign of lack of sophistication. Only when Ngoni falls seriously sick and is taken to his parents' home does he realise the errors of his ways and the shallowness of his wife's values. Rudo does not even bother to visit him while he is ill at his parents' rural home. When Ngoni recovers, he starts clamping down on is wife's vain ways and airs. He buys Shona books and records, he insists that his wife's salary is banked in his name and account in keeping with what he says are African ways. Ngoni says that if Rudo does not want to do as he says, they can get divorced. Rudo chooses to do as her husband says in order to stay married.

VaTamai, Ngoni's mother is also portrayed as a less than ideal wife to VaMasvinyange, her husband. She objects to her husband spending money to send Ngoni to school. When Ngoni writes to tell his parents that he has eye trouble, she tries to get him to take Ngoni out of school altogether. She taunts her husband and calls him a senseless old man who forced her son to go to school where he was bewitched by jealous people. She asks him what school her son will attend when he is already blind. When Ngoni eventually gets spectacles to correct his short sight, Tamai, with the advice of the diviner/medicine man, confiscates Ngoni's spectacles, since she is told they they would interfere with the medicine prescribed. When Ngoni gets disinterested and neglects his parents, VaTamai blames her husband for having insisted on sending Ngoni to school against her advice.

In *Rurimi Inyoka* VaTigere is portrayed as a reasonable man while his wife Madezvipi, Simon's mother is very cruel to her daughter-in-law. Simon's mother causes upheaval and discord in the home by her plots and machinations to get Vida chased away by Simon. Her husband VaTigere knows exactly what his wife is capable of and he tries to moderate her excesses when it comes to interference in the marriage of Vida and Simon. On one occasion VaTigere threatens to chase away Madezvipi herself at her advanced age if she does not stop bothering Vida.

In *Ndakakutadzirei* Mazvironda, the wife of VaShoperai is depicted as a cruel and inconsiderate woman. She tries to discourage her husband from sending his son by his first wife to school. She illtreats Shongedzai the stepdaughter-in-law, till the latter leaves to go to work elsewhere. Mazvironda hates all her husband's relatives. Her husband's brother Dhibha left the home because Mazvironda used to put medicine portions into his food with the intention of harming him. She had also given her daughter Maonzeni some medicine to poison her stepbrother Rwandibva. Generally, she is characterised as a bad person.

In *Sara Ugarike* Marujata's mother VaMaidei is shown to have been a bad wife to her husband whom she had fed a love portion to make him obedient to her. She says this portion was left by her own mother. VaMaidei then passes the portion to her own daughter Marujata so that she can feed it to Mukomondera, her husband, to make sure he is her slave who will never 'raise his head' after he has been fed the portion.

Marujata herself is a flirt and immodest. She asks Kurimahufamba whether he is married. This kind of behaviour is intolerable in a woman, particularly one who is married. She starts an affair with Kurima and is seen by her husband's friend Munhukwaye. Mukomondera is surprised and disappointed and wonders whether he should commit suicide so that Marujata can live her life freely. His friend tells him not to think along those lines since everybody would laugh at him for committing suicide because of a woman. Munhukwaye tells Mukomondera that there is no man who can manage a woman. He says it is not only the wives of poor men who have affairs and commit adultery but also the wives of rich men who even have affairs with their cooks. He says infidelity is the disease of women. Mukomondera goes home and confronts Marujata with the information given to him by Munhukwaye. He beats up Marujata and she goes back to her home. When the quarrel is taken to the village elders, Mukomondera fails to provide convincing evidence that his wife had an affair. All his evidence is based on rumours and hearsay so the court orders him to give his wife a cock for beating her up on the basis of rumours and mere suspicion.

After the quarrel, Mukomondera comes home while Marujata is busy entertaining her lover Kurima. She gets Kurima to leave but he is seen by Mukomondera. Since the husband is drunk, he apologises and asks for food. She gives him *mahewu* to drink saying she had not cooked that day. That night Mukomondera falls ill with aches in his stomach and dies. While Marujata is a widow, she continues her affair with Kurima against custom which requires her to be celibate for a year till the anniversary of her husband's death. This angers her husband's relatives since customarily her behaviour is regarded as defiling her husband's grave. While the affair is on, Marujata's brother-in-law surprises Kurima in Marujata's hut. They fight and Kurima kills the brother-in-law of Marujata and throws his body into a river. Marujata elopes to Kurima's home only to find that Kurima has not divorced his wife as he had promised Marujata. Marujata then stays on as Kurima's second wife by common law.

As Kurima's wife, life is not easy for her since she quarrels with his first wife constantly. During a fight started because Marujata had stolen meat from Ndaizivei, the first wife's pot, Marujata has her nose and her upper lip bitten by Ndaizivei. She is permanently disfigured. Kurima gets arrested for stealing sheep on the farm where he works.

Marujata and Ndaizivei are thrown off the farm. They go to live with Kurima's parents who do not like or accept Marujata. They wait for Kurima to finish serving his jail sentence. When Kurima gets out of prison, he hears that the body of Togara, Marujata's brother-in-law has been found and that the police and relatives of Togara are seeking the murderer. Kurima goes to his parents' home, bids his son goodbye and tries to kill Marujata before he commits suicide. It turns out that Marujata does not die but is already ill with leprosy. She confesses to the police that she poisoned her husband and helped to kill Togara. She stays at the hospital for leprosy patients for two years. Marujata confesses her sins and is baptised and renamed Mariya Magadharena (Mary Magdalene) the night before she dies in a state of grace.

In *Ndochema Naani?* Munhamo is also characterised as a bad wife. She poisons her husband in order to conduct her affair with Zimwai without interference. Thus Munhamo had been unfaithful to her husband while he was still alive and had caused the suicide of her daughter when her lover proved unfaithful and dishonest.

In *Mary Ponderai* by K. Mutize, Mary refuses to tolerate the beatings administered to her by her husband Maruza. Maruza tells her that he beats her because he loves her. Maruza is so anxious that he makes Mary's life difficult. He comes home late and drinks heavily. He accuses her of being a prostitute and having affairs with other men. Maruza wastes the money he earns on drink and he does not buy furniture for the rent-free house they live in. He does not even bother to pay the most important part of the *roora* that he had been charged i.e. the *rusambo* for uxorial rights over his wife and the cow of motherhood that was due to Mary's mother. Mary gets so frustrated that she fights with her husband, beats and chokes him and tells him that from then on she is Ponderai, his husband and he is Mary. She has reversed their roles and is telling him that he is not man enough to be her husband. She walks out on him and tales all the household goods, including his suits, to spite him. She regrets the time she wasted married to him but quite exceptionally, decides that she still has her life to live.

Muchaneta in *Garandichauya* is the prime example of a problem wife. She embodies most of those negative attributes that have been decribed in most of the problem women discussed here. First, Muchaneta has an affair while she is a married woman staying in her father's home. She flirts with a teacher and carries on an affair with Handisumbe, the storekeeper. Handisumbe eventually gets rid of his wife and continues his affairs with Muchaneta. Muchaneta's husband finds out about Muchaneta's affair and divorces her. She marries Handisumbe who embezzles his employer's money so that he can spend it with Muchaneta. Muchaneta takes most the money that she had advised Handisumbe to keep in his house and elopes with Zikomu, the domestic worker Handisumbe had hired for her. Handisumbe is jailed for theft and serves his sentence. Meanwhile Muchaneta had fled with Zikomu to Gatooma (Kadoma). Muchaneta meets Matamba, a young man in Gatooma and she poisons Zikomu so that she can live with Matamba. In Gatooma, Muchaneta had changed her name to Raiza (Liza) and she starts living with Matamba.

Matamba hears that his grandmother has died and decides to go back to his rural home to find out about the cattle he is supposed to inherit from his grandmother. He promises to go and sell the twenty-five head of cattle and bring the money to spend with Muchaneta. When Matamba arries home he finds the twenty-five cattle but cannot sell them because his grandmother had specified that they should be used to pay *roora* for Matamba's wife. Matamba is reluctant to marry a peasant woman since he thinks rural women are not smart or clean and cannot cook food the way he likes it. He is concerned about Muchaneta, the woman he had left in Gatooma. Matamba then meets Tsitsi, a beautiful girl and marries her. After the marriage, Tsitsi gets pregnant and Matamba starts neglecting her and behaving badly. He decides to go back to Gatooma and resumes his affair with Muchaneta. Matamba stays for two years in Gatooma without communicating with his wife Tsitsi. Tsitsi decides to go to Gatooma to find out what has happened to Matamba. She finds Matamba living with Muchaneta. Matamba disowns Tsitsi and Tsitsi is assaulted by both Matamba and Muchaneta. Tsitsi comes back home and reports the whole affair to her mother-in-law. She stays with her mother-in-law for a year until she decides to go back to her father's home. Muchaneta was not pleased by the scene that resulted from Tsitsi's visit and one day while Matamba is at work, she absconds with Matamba's money, household goods, clothes and personal effects. Muchaneta writes an insolent letter to Matamba before she leaves. In the letter she addresses him as the son of a witch and tells him that she has not forgotten what he did to her and that she has fixed him because he thinks he is smart. She asks him to follow her if he is galled by what she has done. She signs off 'What has not been brought by an emissary is lost' meaning that he had not married her so he had no formal grounds for demanding back the goods or property he has spent of given to her. Muchaneta goes to Harare after setting up Matamba for a beating by the boyfriend she is now staying with. Matamba is blinded by the man and his friends who then tell Muchaneta that they have killed Matamba.

In Harare, Muchaneta enjoys herself initially but eventually, her conscience catches up with her. She starts having nightmares about all the men she had had killed or maimed. She starts drinking heavily to escape the nightmares but this actually intensifies her condition. She contracts a skin disease which ruins her face. She is broke and destitute. One day she is recognised by Muchazvirega, the teacher she had had an affair with a long time back and from whom she had run away, owing him twenty pounds. Muchazvirega turns out to be one of the men who had assaulted Matamba and left him for dead. Muchazvirega then assaults Muchaneta and blinds her in one eye. After that Muchaneta is kept by a man who picks her up after her assault. This man is mean and stingy and does not give her a penny for food. He assaults her for no reason when he comes home drunk. Muchaneta stays with him because she has nowhere and nobody to go to. One day a man who turns out to be Handisumbe offers to look after her. She agrees to leave the cruel man she was living with without knowing that this new man who has offered to look after her is Handisumbe. She leaves her husband and is taken to a deserted place out of town by Handisumbe. He reveals his identify to her and then proceeds to blind her in her other eye, cuts off her lips, slits her throat and throws away her head. Handisumbe gets arrested a few days later and is sentenced to death for murdering Muchaneta. The author comments that Muchaneta got her just deserts.

In the Ndebele literature, problem wives also abound. In *Umzenzi Kakhalelwa*, MaSibanda is a bad wife because she neglects her husband while pursuing her religious activities. It turns out that MaSibanda has been practising witchcraft and has harmed her husband with it. She is criticised by her sons and her husband's friends who actually see her leaving her sick husband unfed and generally uncared for.

In *Kutheni* Ntombiyehlazo epitomises the bad wife. She tricks her husband into marrying her by telling him that she is pregnant from him. She turns out not to be pregnant and causes a rift between Ntonga, her husband, and his family. When they get to Gwelo (Gweru), she starts neglectig Ntonga and feeds him a portion that weakens him and makes him ill. When Ntonga gets seriously ill, she does not bother about him but continues to go out, without even telling him where she is going. She discourages him from consulting diviners for fear that they might expose her role in his illness. She says in her family her father and mother do not dabble in traditional medicine and divining and yet her father was renowned for his suspicious activities in witchcraft and her mother was responsible for procuring the medicine that had rendered Ntombi sterile. In fact, Ntonga's parents had objected to his marriage because of his wife's family's shady background and reputation in witchcraft. Ntombi goes to the extent of calling Ntonga a grave, spitting at his face, accusing him of being castrated and unable to give her a child. Sometimes she refuses to cook for him and Ntonga has to do the cooking himself and then he wakes her up to eat. He grows nostalgic for his home and decides to go back there. While Ntonga is gone, their house in Gwelo is broken into but Ntombi never even appears or cares. When Ntonga is cured, his family takes her family to court in the village and they get divorced. Ntonga's family's cattle are turned to them.

In *Ukungazi Kufanalokufa*, Nomalanga is the bad wife. She flees home to live with Jojo in Bulawayo after her father has refused to let him marry her. The father's tribalistic objection is that Jojo was not a Fengu like Nomalanga. However, when Nomalanga gets to town, she falls in with bad company, MaNdlovu, who teaches her a lot of bad ways such as drinking and going about with men who are not her husband. Nomalanga eventually leaves her husband Jojo in Bulawayo and goes to

Salisbury (Harare) where she stays with Dlodlo, her friend MaNdlovu's uncle. Nomalanga starts an affair with Dlodlo and this results in Dlodlo divorcing his wife for Nomalanga. Meanwhile in Bulawayo, Jojo is taken to court by Nomalanga's father and charged with cohabiting with Nomalanga without her father's consent, without marrying her and lastly for throwing her out after he has got tired of her. Jojo is fined twenty dollars.

In Salisbury, Nomalanga stays with Dlodlo for a few months before she disappears only to surface again in Umtali (Mutare). Dlodlo is quite annoyed by this. Nomalanga stays in Umtali but has to leave because she hears that there are women who want to kill her for going around and having affairs with their husbands. She moves to Rusape and Macheke until she decides to go back to Salisbury despite the fact that Dlodlo is looking for her. When she gets to Salisbury, she meets Dlodlo as the station. Dlodlo takes her home straight away and beats her up. Nomalanga persuades Dlodlo to let her be since she has decided to come back to him of her own accord. She sweet-talks Dlodlo and he takes her back, believing that she loves him. Dlodlo then goes to Bulawayo on business and when he returns he discovers that Nomalanga is not at home. He finds her at a pub sitting with three men, one of whom has his arms around her. A fight ensues when the men refuse to let Nomalanga go with Dlodlo. Dlodlo is stabbed to death in the fight. Nomalanga finds another man Shoti who spends a lot of money on her. After Shoti is sacked from work because he had been jailed and fined for causing a fight in a pub while protecting Nomalanga, Nomalanga ditches him and moves to another township. She stays there and thinks she has got rid of Shoti. One day she meets him in a nightclub in Highfields and pretends not to recognise him because she is with other men. Shoti persists in talking to Nomalanga and claims her as his wife until Nomalanga gets angry and starts assaulting Shoti. Shoti then stabs Nomalanga with a knife and she dies.

In *Akulazulu Emhlabeni*, Grace Mpofu and her mother MaNkala are both depicted as bad wives. MaNkala is indulgent of her adulterous daughter Grace. This angers Grace's father so much that he beats the fat MaNkala when she intervenes in a conversation between Grace and her father. Mpofu feels that it is the indulgent MaNkala who encourages Grace to behave in an unwifely manner to her husband, Ndebele.

Grace herself is first introduced to the reader as a querulous wife, complaining about the train, the change of job and the boys dancing in the waiting room. By Chapter Two we learn that Grace is having an affair with a man who is married. Grace derelicts on her wifely duties. Her husband comes home and finds no lunch ready while Grace is sleeping. Grace talks rudely to her husband when he tells her about a temporary job. The result is that he beats her up. Time passes until Grace finds a temporary job as a nurse in Dr Makhenzi's (Mackenzie) surgery. She finds it easy to phone her boyfriend in Gwelo. Grace's boyfriend advises her to divorce her husband. He suggests that she should behae in an annoying and provocative fashion to her husband so that he can find a reason to divorce her. Grace then goes to drink before she gets home from work. Her husband, Ndebele merely observes all Grace's deeds without taking any action. When the phone rings at the surgery, Grace picks it up and assumes that it is her boyfriend calling. She starts talking in lovey-dovey fashion, saying she no longer loves her husband and had started doing things that are calculated to annoy him. The call is cut off before she can finish her conversation. The person on the other end is her husband Ndebele who is surprised to discover that his wife has a lover. The same evening Grace comes home drunk, her clothes in tatters, her dress zip open and her underwear showing. Her shoes are in her hands and she is walking in her stockings. Her hair is dusty and she is being pursued by another woman who is fighting her and calling her a prostitute. Grace's mother's brother happens to be there when all this takes place and he gets so disgusted that he leaves after telling Grace what he thinks of her behaviour. Grace continues drinking until one day she gets so drunk that she cannot get herself home and spends the night at a police station. Her husband thrashes her when she gets home. Grace waits for her husband to go to work then she packs her clothes, takes her children and heads for her father's house in Gwelo. Grace lies to her father about the circumstances surrounding her departure from Bulawayo, saying that her husband does not sleep at home or give her housekeeping money, that he beats her when she asks where he has been.

In Bulawayo, Ndebele discovers that Grace had flooded the whole house with water, cut up all the shirts to pieces, broken all the china in the display cabinet and the cabinet itself, smashed Ndebele's typewriter, drenched the mealie meal with water and generally destroyed all the property she could not take with her. In Gwelo, Grace had a lovely time with her lover. When Ndebele follows her to Gwelo to bring her back, she refuses to go back. She files for a divorce and then discovers that she is pregnant from Moyo her lover. Moyo is worried and decides that Grace should try to procure an abortion. Grace goes to a doctor and tells him her problem. He promises to help her but phones her husband instead and congratulates him on his wife's expectation. The doctor happens to know Ndebele through friends of his and he keeps Ndebele posted about Grace's condition. Grace gets worried when her pregnancy gets more and more visible. Grace's lover starts shunning her when he sees the affair getting more complicated as a result of Grace's pregnancy. The lover cheats Grace by not divorcing his wife as Grace expected him to do. Grace attends the court hearing where it becomes apparent that her husband does not illtreat her. He refuses to grant her a divorce and files a charge of adultery against Grace on the grounds that she is pregnant from another man. Grace realises that she is in trouble because the doctor has cheated her and Moyo is also not being honest about his stand with regard to her. She confronts Moyo at a public beer garden. Moyo is arrogant and contemptuous towards Grace. He says he has nothing to do with her pregnancy. Their quarrel develops into a fight and Grace stabs Moyo with a knife. Grace is taken into police custody and serves a six month jail sentence for stabbing Moyo. Grace's husband then divorces her and gets custody of their children. Her father refuses to look after her so she has to go to her mother's brother's home. Her lover absconds with his family to Salisbury and her aunt who had looked after her while she was separated from Ndebele has moved to Filabusi. Her mother cannot do much to help her. In the end, Grace is isolated and abandoned by all the people she had cared for including those who had encouraged her to break up her marriage.

We need to analyse the images presented of wives in the novels and stories cited above. The most recurrent images are those of adulteresses, poisoners and cruel women. They castrate their husbands verbally and then go ahead to cuckold, poison, beat up and generally embarrass their husbands in many ways. This view of women is repeated by the male characters such as Old Makiwa, Zakeo's grandfather, Munhukwaye in *Sara Ugarike*, the two men talking at the station in *Garandichauya* and the author's editorial in *Garandichauya*, to mention but a few examples.

The women themselves are treated in a particular way by the authors. Most of the women who are not bad are described in a nebulous and physically unspecific fashion. For example, Vida in *Rurimi Inyoka* is introduced as a person with a kind heart. We are not told how she looks or how tall or short she is. Tsitsi in *Garandichauya* is described as being slim with a flattish nose and slightly tall. We are told that her dress fitted her nicely. The individual features described are not put into a composite whole that allows us to 'see' her. Shongedzai in *Ndakakutadzirei* and Ndaizivei in *Sara Ugarike* are not described either. The good woman are non-sexual and have no physical presence either. In contrast, the wicked domineering women are described vividly either to imply their grossness or prettiness so that we can follow how their looks deteriorate or are ruined by people these women have harmed. Mazvironda in *Ndakakutadzirei* is described as *gadzi*, a large woman and throughout the book, we are reminded of her grossness. MaNkala, Mpofu's wife in *Akulazulu Emhlabeni* is described as a fat woman who would be a problem to get to the cemetery the day she died. Later in the book while her husband is beating her up, she is described as being so full of fat that she is the size of a granary. The author says it was as if Mpofu were lashing an elephant with straws. When Mpofu sees how ineffectual his beating is, he decides to go for her neck with both hands to throttle her. All this information is calculated to emphasise MaNkala's grossness. In *Garandichauya*, Muchaneta's physical beauty is described graphically, she smells nicely, dresses well and provokes with her body and its movements. She is one of the few women in the vernacular literature who is characterised as a sex-symbol. It is useful for the authors to describe the bad, wicked wives and women because when retribution is dished out, the reader can also be called upon to revel in the destruction of the bodies and source of confidence of these women.

Muchaneta is mutilated by one of her lovers and goes blind in one eye. The author then traces the decline of Muchaneta's looks and fortunes. Another vengeful ex-lover looks for her and finds her in Harare and blinds her in the remaining eye, severs her lips (for 'eating' men's money) slits her throat and throws away her head. In *Sara Ugarike*, Marujata is also mutilated by Kurima's first wife in the course of a fight. She has her upper lip and nose bitten, develops a skin disease and is diagnosed to be suffering from leprosy. She is ugly by the time she dies. Another bad woman Lifile in S. Mlilo's *Lifile* comes back to mourn her mother. Lifile has become sterile because of the venereal disease she contracted and kept untreated for a long time. She is characterised as a 'shell' because she cannot bear children, feel labour pains or be chaffed by the straps of a baby carrier. Grace in *Akulazulu Emhlabeni*, cuts a miserable figure when she gets out of prison. Her clothes are wrinkled, she has grown thin and miserable because nobody except her mother wants her.

The prevalence of the theme of adultery also reveals the preoccupation of most writers who are male. All the female writers whose works are examined do not dwell on the theme of adultery as the central point of conflict between men and women. Most of the male writers do so. The infidelity of women, be they wives or girlfriends is the preoccupation of the male writers. Most of the male writers are very concerned about the control over women's sexuality. It is the women who decide what to do with their sexuality, against customary dictates, who are punished most severely, preferably with death. Cases in point are Marujata, Muchaneta and Jane. The other women who do not necessarily commit adultery but are bad in other ways also get their deserts. The tough, big ones are tenderised by beatings, remorse, poverty and the realisation that they were mistaken. Cases in point are MaNkala who is beaten by her husband and isolated from her adulterous daughter. MaSibanda is exposed as a witch and is forced to kill her familiars and confess all her misdeeds. Marujata and Muchaneta's mothers die destitute and their adulterous daughters do not even take care of them in their old age. Munhamo, the adulterous wife of Zindoga is sentenced to death.

In contrast to wives, erring husbands do not suffer such drastic fates. Moyo, Grace's lover, does not die when Grace stabs him but he has his loving wife to go back to. Matamba gets blinded but he has a wife who is all sweetness and light, ready to welcome him back with open arms. Maruza, Mary's husband continues his life after his wife leaves him. Rwandibva has a loving wife who forgives him for all the cruelty and bad treatment he has put her through. However, lovers or married women do suffer in the hands of the authors who exert control over the means of violence and retribution. Kurima, Zimwai and Handisumbe are sentenced to death by the state. However, they are not killed by vengeful, deceived female lovers and in a way, they are redeemed by the fact that they are seen to be paying their debts to society. Moyo, Grace's lover goes back to his wife while Timothy, the deceitful lover of Jane is killed in a fight with Jane's brother. Women never try to get their revenge on deceiving lovers and when they do, they fail as Grace did with Moyo. Ultimately, it is the state or other agencies whom they have to rely on to avenge them.

******

There is a difference between the characterisation of wives and women by authors writing in English and those writing in the vernacular. As has been indicated in the descriptions of women as mothers and wives, the writers in English are generally more sophisticated and less stereotypic in their characterisation of women. The women characters in English works, are more sensitively drawn and explored. A good example to illustrate the point is drawing of the relationships between parents and children. In the vernacular works, almost all the daughters who turn out to be bad wives and mothers also had bad mothers themselves. The only exception is

Ntombi, in Eunice Mthethwa's *Kutheni* Ntombi's father is also characterised as an unsavoury character who has been involved in seducing and murdering another villager's daughter and has managed to get away with it. Ncube, Ntombi's father is also known to be involved in witchcraft activities. Ntombi's mother may have been instrumental in getting Ntombi 'fixed' so that she can escape the consequences of premarital sex but she is not villified out of proportion to the other characters. In mist of the other Shona and Ndebele novels, most bad wives and daughters have a mother in alliance with them and most bad mothers and wives have a daughter in apprenticeship to them. While the same threads may be evident in the English works, the characters who are targets and victims of wives' badness are also explored and their weaknesses exposed.

In Mungoshi's 'The day the bread van didn't come', we are shown not only Mrs Pfende's badness but her husband's meanness and general weakness as a person. In 'The Victim', we see Mangazva's mother's dominance as well as her son's spinelessness and wickedness towards his own wife. In 'Who will stop the dark?' we see Zakeo's mother as both a strong determined woman as well as a frustrated mother who loves her son. Even her father-in-law realises that she is right in her plans to rear her son for his world despite the fact that the old man himself disapproves of Zakeo's mother. In Nyamfukudza's 'Guilt and Sorrow', the woman recognises that her paternal grandmother was a weak woman who may have influenced her son likewise. At the same time, she loves her father despite his weakness and her mother for her strength. The woman realises how anxious and threatened her husband feels because she has a job and she tempers her judgement and attitude towards him. Makhalisa's 'Baby-snatcher' also explores the complexity of Ntombi's motivation while exposing her husband's weakness.

These differences are partly attributable to the differential development of prose and the novel in English and in the vernacular in Zimbabwe. It is also signal to note that the pre-independence regime had a literature bureau which censored, shaped and selected writings that were simple, unproblematic and apolitical for publication. Makhalisa's writings in Ndebele prior to independence do resemble the vernacular ones cited in this book. A lot of the authors of Shona and Ndebele are either Christian or conservative traditionalists or both and have been school teachers for a long time. They are the ones who were leaders in the literacy field and were in a position to push a strong disciplinary and conservative moral stance in their writings.

Notwithstanding the explanations for the literary style of vernacular writings, the point still remains that he oversimplification of issues and characterisations gives rise to stereotype images of women. C. Mungoshi's *Kunyarara Hakusi Kutaura?* a Shona work, is quite sophisticated in style and characterisation and escapes the stereotypic tradition of characterisation of women in general, wives in particular. This work is not 'political' but it is sensitive to all the characters involved and accomplishes the point of exploring and explaining the feelings of the characters involved sensitively.

Notes to Chapter 2: Women as wives

1. page 30, *Some Kinds of Wounds,* Mambo Press, 1980.
2. page 41, *ibid.*
3. page 45, *ibid.*
4. page 124, *ibid.*
5. page 127, *ibid.*
6. page 128, *ibid.*
7. page 142, *ibid.*
8. page 147, *ibid.*
9. page 147, *ibid.*
10. page 166, *ibid.*
11. page 167, *ibid.*
12. page 167, *ibid.*
13. page 169, *ibid.*
14. page 176, *ibid.*
15. page 38, *Aftermaths,* The College Press, 1983.
16. page 36, *ibid.*
17. page 42, *ibid.*

3

Women without husbands

In some of the works cited in this book, there are women who for one reason or another are without husbands. However, there are times and instances where women stay with men in the way legally married people do. The unions may be unregistered and *roora* unpaid but the couples may actually regard each other as husbands and wives. A good example of this is the relationship between Marujata and Kurima in *Sara Ugarike*, Nomalanga and Jojo in *Ukungazi Kufana Lokufa* and Muchaneta and Matamba in *Garandichauya*. Why concentrate on the marital aspect with relation to women who are on their own? This is because the way adult women are often defined is in relation to men as husbands. Some readers may find this line of definition and analysis objectionable on the basis that it conforms to the definitions reserved for women and they way women are supposed to relate to men. However, the point is not whether one agrees with this definition or not but to realise that the way the images of women in the literature are drawn, there is very little legitimacy for adult women's existence without husbands. An examination of the writings is necessary to illustrate this point.

There are categories of women without men and their images differ according to the reasons for their husbandless status. There are widows, divorces, single, jilted women, women who have joined religious order e.g. nuns and women who have failed or do not want to secure a man in marriage or consensual union.

Widows

Widows are usually older women although we do find some relatively younger women such as Marujata. Among the widowed women are such characters as VaNdakanatswa, Rwandibva's paternal grandmother in *Ndakakutadzirei*, Mhurai's grandmother in *Ndochema Naani?*, Muchaneta's mother and Matamba's grandmother in *Garandichauya*, Marujata's mother VaMaidei in *Sara Ugarike*,

Munhamo in *Ndochema Naani?* and VaChingweru, Monica's mother in *Makunun'unu Maodzamwoyo*. In the Ndebele works there are widows such as Lifile's mother in *Lifile*, and Ntombiyezwe's grandmother in *Wangithengisela Umntanakhe*. Most of the widowed women are above child bearing age and as such are not even supposed to entertain thoughts of remarriage or sexual relationships with men. Most have grandchildren and have attained the role of advisers to all their children and grandchildren. In most patrilineal societies, women attain more power and influence with age especially over their granddaughters. Maternal grandmothers are said to be important to women over child bearing and fertility matters when the grandmothers have died and become ancestors. As long as widows are not suspected of having hastened the deaths of their husbands, they are accorded high status and respect in the homes of their children, particularly sons. However, widows like Marujata are not highly respected since they are suspected of having been unfaithful to their husbands before widowhood. Young widows are allowed to remarry as long as they fulfill the customary obligations towards their deceased husbands. Marujata failed to do this since she had an affair with a lover before the year's mourning period for her husband was over. Young widows can also opt to be inherited by the brothers of their deceased husbands if the brothers-in-law are willing.

Since marriage is viewed as necessary for procreation rather than personal pleasure, widows beyond childbearing age run the risk of being stigmatised should they desire to remarry. People ask what the point of such marriages is. In any case, most widows would not like to go elsewhere to start afresh in another man's patrilineage as new daughters-in-law without status or influence. Status and influence go with motherhood and age so most widows opt to stay with the deceased husband's family especially if they have had a number of sons. Widows can then expect to be looked after by their sons or grandchildren when they grow old. Thus widows who have been good and faithful wives are accorded high respect and can expect to be looked after by their sons or grandchildren in their husband's patrilineages. The situation outlined above applies in the novels and stories cited above. However, there are situations where widows can refuse to be inherited or where elderly widows may desire remarriage even when they can no longer bear children. These situations are not outlined or presented in the literature examined in this book and this can be questioned and discussed. However, one can say that generally, widows are accorded high respect as long as they have been good and faithful wives during their husbands lifetimes and if they continue to be celibate or to behave in the customarily expected manner after their husband's death. Deceased husbands' relatives can get resentful if widows have affairs or relationships with other men even after the mourning period is over. Under certain circumstances outlined above, widows can expect respect from society in general and deceased husbands' relatives in particular.

Widows can also expect some pity or commiseration from society. Women without husbands because of death are generaly sympathised with especially if their children are very young or if they have no sons. A man can get another wife but a women past her prime cannot do the same with equal ease. There is the feeling that women cannot possibly manage without husbands and this is true to some extent for those widows who are dependent on their husbands' patrilineages for land, material support or help. In rural Zimbabwe this is usually the case. Most women who live in town and are dependent on husbands' wages are also in a precarious position and have to depend on their children or find waged jobs. Most widows particularly the older ones are not usually educated or skilled in any waged occupation and can be very dependent on children or deceased husbands' kin. This effectively curtails widows' freedom to act whichever way they would like to since their dependence carries with it obligations to behave in ways acceptable to the people who support them.

Divorced women

Divorced women also appear in the literature dealt with in this work. Generally, the image of the divorced woman is very negative. The only exceptions in terms of negative characterisation for divorced women are those whose husbands obviously illtreat them and divorce them because of the influence of or to marry, bad women. Tsitsi and Handisumbe's wife in *Garandichauya*, Dlodlo's wife in *Ukungazi Kufana Lokufa* and Runesu's wife in Tsodzo's play *Tsano* are good wives who have been divorced or sent away because their husbands are influenced by and involved in affairs with wicked women. However, the characters in the literature do express their views about divorced women.

VaTigere, Simon's father threatens Simon's mother with divorce if she does not stop interfering with Vida and Simon's marriage. MaMthombeni, Ntonga's mother in *Kutheni* wants Ntombi divorced because she is childless. Ntombi is so afraid of being divorced that she consults her mother for help so that she can have a child. VaChingweru considers her daughter Tendai a prostitute because Tendai is divorced. Mary Ponderai's aunt tried to persuade Mary to stay with her husband. Mary says she is not afraid of being called a loose woman, the term used to refer to women who have not made a success of marriage, women who have more than one relationship with a man, or women who are judged to be fickle and casual in their relationships with men. In *Umzenzi Kakhalelwa*, MaSibanda mocks MaNyathi's daughter who has come back from her husband's home because their marriage was not successful. Grace Mpofu is divorced and unwanted even by her father. Like widows, divorced women can be seen as respectable as long as they behave in customarily approved ways before and after divorce. It is usually the husbands who divorce wives and the reasons for the divorce determine how the divorced women are treated and regarded. Generally, the women who are divorced because of the bad behaviour of their husbands are regarded well. This non-condemning attitude can change if the women behave in a loose or otherwise unacceptable way subsequent to their divorce.

A lot of wives will opt to stay with husbands even if the husbands illtreat them. Ndaizivei in *Sara Ugarike* stays on as Kurima's wife even when Kurima brings Marujata home without warning Ndaizivei. A lack of alternatives for women without husbands partly accounts for women's reluctance to divorce even when the marriage is stressful. Socially, it is felt that a wife's place is with her husband and divorce is a sign of failure for the woman in particular since it proves that she cannot use her womanly wiles and virtues to keep her husband contented with her. Thus women are judged by their ability to get a man and keep him. This partly explains why women are so scared of divorce and the image of them that society will hold after the divorce.

The welfare of children also has a lot of influence on women who might contemplate divorce. Shona and Ndebele societies are patrilineal and the payment of *roora* assures husbands' lineages of custody over the children in a marriage. A woman who leaves her married home also loses custody over her children who are beyond infancy if her husband has paid *roora*. For example, Grace loses custody of her children to Ndebele. Elsewhere in this work, the image of the stepmother has been shown to be negative because stepmothers are seen as cruel, heartless, jealous and more than likely to illtreat the children of a husband's former wife. Most women therefore opt to stay and look after their children even if the marriage is unsuccessful and unsatisfactory. By the time children grow up and get independent, most women have little incentive to leave their husbands to start life all over as divorced or remarried women.

Thus the stigmatisation of divorce, the concern for children's welfare and the dependence on husbands for means of gaining a living through the land or waged jobs, makes women reluctant to leave a bad marriage. In the cases of Tsitsi, Ndaizivei and Runesu's wife, the behaviour of their husbands led them to separate from their husbands only to go and stay with the husbands' parents. Thus these women moved from dependence on the husbands to dependence on the husbands' parents. In Tsitsi's case, she eventually went back to her own father's home and was partly dependent on him. Ndaizivei stays with Kurima's parents while Handisumbe's wife got married to another man. Runesu's wife and her husband probably got reconciled but the point that divorced women find it difficult to live life without greatly depending on men still stands. In this respect, they are in a similar situation to the widows dealt with earlier in this book.

Single women

For the purposes of definition, single women are considered to be those women who have never married legally or in consensual unions. By this definition, women like Nomalanga Jola can be regarded as having married although the consensual union is later dissolved when Nomalanga absconds to Salisbury. After leaving Jojo, Nomalanga stays with Dlodlo in another consensual union before leaving him and living the life of a single woman. Muchaneta also does the same after leaving Matamba although the duration of her 'single' life is quite short. Other examples of single women are Lifile who cohabits with a man until he throws her out after giving her a thrashing. Lifile then wanders around town staying with whoever will accommodate her until she goes to the infectious diseases hospital to be treated for venereal disease. She is unable to attend her father's funeral while in hospital. In the end, she goes back to her Uncle's rural home for good. She is pitied and mocked because her boyfriend has found another girl. Lifile is sterile and will probably never find a husband since no man would want a woman who has been to town and cannot bear children because of her promiscuity while in town.

Jane in *Rurimi Inyoka* is also a single women who strives hard to find a man to marry her. She is jilted by Simon who prefers Vida and this hurts and humiliates her. The neighbours laugh at her and speculate on the reasons why she was jilted. They encourage her attempts to 'capture' back Simon while he is married to Vida. Jane fails because Simon is not interested in her. Jane meets Timothy in Harare and takes up with him. Timothy just wants to sleep with Jane so he treats her nicely while they are in Harare. He promises to marry her, then Jane goes back to her rural home ecstatic and ready to apologise to Vida for all the bad treatment she had subjected Vida to. Timothy gets sacked from his job in town and goes back to his rural home. Jane gets pregnant by Timothy and expects Timothy to marry her as he has promised. Timothy gets influenced against Jane by Mai Zipfende and Mai Mashumba. He had intended to marry Jane after discovering that Jane was pregnant but the things said by Mai Zipfende and Mai Mashumba about Jane set him thinking again. They tell him that it was a bad idea for a proper man like him to marry a woman who had been jilted by his friend. They liken Jane to vomit that had been thrown up by another man, a blanket that has been used by another man. They remind him that Jane has come to him only after she had been turned away by Simon in Harare and ask why Timothy is willing to accept a woman who has been found nauseous by another man. They tell him that Jane is a prostitute since a proper, respectable woman would never go to look for men in their houses. They advise Timothy to deny responsibility for Jane's pregnancy on the grounds that she is a prostitute. They tell him that if he marries her, the whole world would bubble with laughter and Jane would probably continue in her whorish ways even after marrying him.

Timothy takes the advice of the two women and in court he calls Jane a prostitute and refuses to marry her. He asks the court whether it would fault any hyena that ate up a goat that was placed in its lair meaning that Jane had come to his house, something a decent woman would never dream of doing. The court finds Jane culpable and exonerates Timothy from responsibility for Jane. She is so ashamed and humiliated that she commits suicide. Jane's brother Tobias, kills Timothy by choking him and Tobias himself dies from stab wounds inflicted on him by Timothy during their fight. Thus Jane's case shows how single women are regarded especially if they are deemed to be behaving improperly. Jane is humiliated by the fact that she had been jilted by Simon. Her life becomes difficult and she is so desperate to demonstrate that she can get a man and keep him that she is willing to risk her reputation by sleeping with Timothy before he has married her. However, the stigma resulting from her jilting by Simon causes Timothy to renege on his promise to marry her. Timothy does not want to be seen to be consorting with a woman who has been jilted by another man.

Lifile in *Lifile* is another single woman who lost a potential husband because she behaved in a disapproved fashion by running away to town. Her boyfriend Thando is encouraged by other people to find another woman of better morals since Lifile is considered a prostitute for having gone to town where people were said to be immoral and badly behaved. Thando then starts associating with Bahle, Lifile's best friend. Bahle is keen to become Thando's wife but Thando takes his time proposing and he does not commit himself to Bahle either way. In the end, Bahle feels humiliated when Thando finally decides to marry Sithembile instead.

Anatoria Tichafa (We will die) is a nurse who is jilted by her boyfriend Josiah after he discovers that she is pregnant. Anatoria has fallen in love with Josiah after Josiah pretends to be a Christian. Anatoria is a Christian herself and she thinks that Josiah will stick to his promise to marry her should she fall pregnant. Anatoria is a virgin when Josiah first sleeps with her. After Anatoria gets pregnant, Josiah tells her that she is a prostitute and he had no intention of marrying her since he his other girlfriends who are better and more qualified to marry him than Anatoria. Anatoria waits until she has borne her child, a girl named Rudo Moyo, then she commits suicide because of her shame and heartbreak.

Her daughter Rudo grows up a good girl. She is raised by a missionary since her mother Anatoria was an orphan with no relatives. Rudo gets pregnant by a man who had also impregnated and jilted Anatoria. Joe, (Josiah) illtreats Rudo while she stays with him. One day she lets him take too many sleeping tablets while he is drunk and then reveals her identify to him. Joe dies and Rudo starts her life afresh after getting a two year suspended jail sentence because it was not clear whether Joe had died from heart disease or from an overdose of sleeping tablets. The illtreatment of Rudo and her mother by Joe, her miscarriage after her fight with Joe and Rudo's youth all constitute extenuating circumstances. Rudo then starts her life afresh as a single woman.

Nhlokotshiyane, the daughter of Mabhena, is a single, professional woman. She was a registered nurse and has been disowned by her father for refusing to marry the man chosen for her by her father. After the beating she received from her father, Nhlokotshiyane goes to Bulawayo, buys herself a house and continues with her affair with Johannes, the man of her choice. She works at a hospital and one day she meets her father who has been taken ill at home in the country and has been brought to an urban hospital. She cares for him well and her father relents when he realises that his daughter is operating and living in a different environment from that of her rural home. Nhlokotshiyane is then free to marry the man of her choice.

Nhlokotshiyane's father realises and feels that his daughter needs to get married since she has spent so much time in school while her age-mates were getting married. When Nhlokotshiyane refuses to marry the man her father has chosen, the other wives laugh and revel in the fact that the beloved, jumped-up daughter has finally embarrassed her father as they had predicted. They mock their husband privately for having sent a 'visitor', that is a daughter, to school while the son and heir does not get any schooling. Nhlokotshiyane is not derogated because she had continued to behave correctly, in the way a single woman is expected to behave. She has not cohabited with her boyfriend or married him by civil law as one other girl who is also a nurse has done when her parents refuse to let her marry the man of her choice.

Martha in *Kunyarara Hakusi Kutaura?* is a single woman who is waiting for her boyfriend to propose marriage to her. Martha has had a baby by another man who has refused to marry her. She has a University degree obtained while her boyfriend Eric, was studying in England. She behaves very well, visiting her boyfriend's relatives and buying his mother presents. However, the boyfriend is faithless. He is seen by Martha kissing Lorna, his sister-in-law, on the day Eric and Martha are engaged to be married. Later in London, Martha finds Eric with a white girlfriend who has her arms around Eric. As if that were not enough, Martha also finds love letters to Eric from Lorna. Martha is embittered by all this in view of the fact that Eric does not pay her much attention when he comes back from England. Eric goes to stay with his half brother, Paul and his wife Lorna. Martha vows that she will never visit Eric while he was staying in Lorna's house. Eric continues his affair with Lorna until Paul her husband, discovers it. Lorna then cries rape and Eric is arrested. Lorna commits suicide since she knows what has been happening between herself and Eric. Martha takes comfort in her job and hopes that some man will find her lovable and marry her. She thinks Eric will not marry her after serving his prison sentence since, to Eric, she will be a constant reminder of his misdeeds. She thinks that Eric will go back to England after serving his sentence. Thus like all the other women who are single, Martha becomes a 'lady in waiting', that is, waiting for a man who will come and marry her thus making her a respectable wife and mother.

Soneni in *Ukungazi Kufana Lokufa* used to be Jojo's girlfriend before Jojo met Nomalanga. When Jojo sees Nomalanga, he jilts Soneni telling her that he is not prepared to marry her. He does not tell her the real reason to explain his change of mind but merely states that he is tired of her and is no longer in love with her. He advises her to go her own way and find some other man while she still can. Soneni is heartbroken and disappointed. When Jojo is abandoned by Nomalanga in Bulawayo, he writes back to Soneni asking for forgiveness and telling her that he had been tempted and overpowerd by the devil. He never tells her that he had jilted her for another woman. Soneni is only too ready to forgive him and she hopes he will not do the same thing again. His letter appears quite convincing and she wonders what could have happened to make him say that he was tired of her and no longer loved her. Her trust in him is restored and she forgives him. She had never really believed that their affair was well and truly over. When Jojo proposes marriage she accepts and marries him.

Thandiwe in T.M. Ndlovu's *Ithemba Kalubulali* is another single woman who was jilted by her lover after he had got her pregnant. Thandiwe was sent to school by her parents until she qualified to go to teacher training college. There she meets a young teacher who has an affair with her and gets her pregnant. The teacher, Ndebele, tries to get Thandiwe to name another man as responsible for her pregnancy. Ndebele is trying to avoid implicating himself in the problem of getting a schoolgirl pregnant. He knows that if he is found out, he would run the risk of losing his job, his teaching license or both. Thandiwe accepts the money offered but refuses to name another man as the father of her baby since that would bar the way for Ndebele to marry her. Thandiwe then agrees not to name Ndebele as the father of her baby. Ndebele then promises to continue to support her materially. He tells her he loves her and he assures her that his plan is to make sure he does not lose his job, a problem which would ruin both their lives. After that Ndebele decides not to go to Thandiwe's home with her. Thandiwe is found out by the school authorities while she is waiting to catch a bus home. She refuses to tell who the father of her baby is. She lies to her parents that she has been sent home to recover from an illness and they assume she is going back to school. Thandiwe decides to leave home on the pretext that she is going back to school as her parents ask her to do. She decides to go and work on a farm as a cotton picker till her boyfriend marries her. The boyfriend stops writing to Thandiwe and changes his place of work. Thandiwe has a difficult pregnancy and has a baby on her own at the farm. She decides to abandon the baby but is caught and thrown into jail before she can get far from where the baby is lying abandoned.

Thandiwe's parents are called to her trial where she is sentenced to a year's hard labour in jail or two hundred dollars fine. Thandiwe's parents and brother pay the fine and then sue Ndebele for getting their daughter thrown out of school before she had completed her course and for the expenses incurred by Thandiwe's family at and since the birth of her baby. Ndebele is fined two hundred and twenty five dollars. Ndebele has married another girlfriend after he has transferred to Bulawayo. Thandiwe is left literally holding the baby, an unmarried mother without means of support for herself and her baby because she has no professional qualification. She is seen as an embarrassment to her family on whom she depends for her child's and her own support. She confirms the worst fears of those of her family's neighbours who had always held that sending a daughter to school is a waste of time and money as well as asking for disappointment.

Vimbai, the daughter of Munhamo, is a young girl who is impregnated by her mother's lover who has raped her. Vimbai prefers to commit suicide rather than to live a life of shame as an unmarried mother of Zimwai's child and a rape victim.

In K. Bepswa's *Ndakamuda Dakara Afa*, we see a young single woman who takes the decision to become a nun after her plans to marry her boyfriend Taremba who loved her are frustrated. Taremba's friend Shingirai frustrates the lovers' marriage plans by writing a rude letter to Rujeko's father. Shingirai uses Taremba's name and address so that Rujeko's father stops Rujeko marrying Taremba. Things happen that way and Rujeko, presumably as a result of frustration, becomes a nun. Shingirai goes onto murder sister Ruth, the new name Rujeko has been using since becoming a nun. He burns Rujeko's father's home and implicates Taremba again. In the end, Shingirai is caught and sentenced to death.

In Makhalisa's story 'The Underdog' Netsai, the young woman is sentenced to two years' in jail with hard labour, nine months conditionally suspended for three years, for having an abortion. Netsai had to leave school because of the liberation war raging in her home area. She had to sleep, under duress, with district assistants who worked for the colonial regime. After Independence, she has had to go to work, as a domestic in town, to support her mother, her younger sisters and brothers. She stays with her aunt's husband who rapes her. She leaves his home and finds work as a domestic. Her employer's husband sexually molests her after lending her twenty dollars. Netsai feels obliged to succumb since she feels it hopeless to walk off in high dudgeon only to land up, as was usual and frequent, with another employer who would also make passes or harass her sexually. She discovers she is pregnant a few weeks later and decides to have an abortion so that she can continue working to support her family. She gets so sick with pain that she is taken to hospital where the police take her to court and she is sentenced after her recovery. She is ignored by the man who impregnated her and she is hampered by a criminal record. She loses her boyfriend. Her family is hurt and embarrassed since all the neighbours will talk about her. There is no prospect of a better life for her mother, brothers and sisters after Netsai has lost her job and starts serving her sentence. Thus for single, lowly educated women, life is difficult both in the country and in town.

In 'To Keep Him' by Makhalisa, we meet Mara struggling to keep her boyfriend Dan and to get him to marry her. She tries to get her friend Zodwa who has a 'steady' boyfriend to tell her what charms or medicine to use to keep a boyfriend. Mara uses the best creams and make-up, medicines and charms to try to keep Dan. She fights any girls who date Dan, threatens and scolds them on the phone in order to stop them sneaking Dan from under her nose. Her friend Chipo advises her not to '. . . nag like a leaking tap and across examine him about his other affairs as if he is a prisoner'.[1] Zodwa advises Mara not to be a jealous and resentful especially when on a date with Dan. Mara passes on to Zodwa's flat. In is clear that Mara, the girl without a boyfriend, is lonely and cannot even stand her own empty flat or company. She aims to get supper at Zodwa's so that she will not have to face her own flat and its messy state. She rings Dan and when he does not answer his phone, she rings his other girlfriend's flat to make sure that the other girlfriend is also at home and presumably, not with Dan.[1] She finds out that Mary is at home and hangs up then thinks that Dan might just be with Mary in Mary's flat. Mara is disheartened.

She gets to Zodwa's flat and finds Zodwa baking a cake for her husband. Zodwa advises Mara to leave Dan if he is behaving badly. Zodwa proceeds to lecture her on men, and how they need to be pampered and have their egos boosted '. . . men are both mature children and bossy adults'.[2] Mara tells her that women have to form a strong solidarity and fight for their rights. 'What rights?' asks Zodwa who says she's not a libber and would prefer a more feminine battle than that being fought by some of the so-called libbers. Mara thinks over the fact that she is not young and most of her age-mates are already married. She is afraid of being considered an old maid on the shelf. Mara is depressed by the sight of Zodwa and her husband whose intimacy makes her feel lonely. She then leaves Zodwa's place and gets to her own flat. The first thing she does is to phone Dan who answers the phone and shows no interest in seeing Mara again. Dan advises her to look for another man since he is '. . . fed up with your gush concerning equal rights, especially when I thought I was treating you like a lady. Goodbye.'[3] Thus goes Dan. Mara cries and has a headache the following day. Her boss sends her to see a doctor. Mara goes straight to see a traditional medicine doctor who tells her 'Mh, I can see. Yes, you did not apply the right amount of that powder I gave you, to your washing water. The water was just lukewarm too instead of being fairly hot. Yes. I can see what made things fail. Your young man is still loose, not reigned. There are two courses left for you now, my daughter. One is, I must remove the unlucky spirit that is hovering about you. We have to do it tonight at a pool. I will hve to dip you in it after applying a cleansing powder I have here. So, go home and bring back one of your good dresses which you will never wear again as I shall burn it afterwards.' Mara debates whether to go back again after paying twenty dollars for the consultation and she decides to go to the doctor's ' . . . for she had to fight to keep him.'[4]

Mary Ponderai lives a single life after she starts working on a farm. She has a boyfriend who is the foreman at the farm. She is mentally disturbed and restless because of the thoughts about all the people she has fought with and presumably, killed as Jimmy informs her. Mary goes to see a doctor on her employer's recommendation. The doctor talks to her and gives her some medicine. He assures her that she is only overwrought and should not feel paranoid since she is a good, normal person. Mary feels better, leaves her job and goes to visit her parents in Harare. She meets Sarudzai an old friend whom she had presumed dead, from Jimmy's information. She is told by Sarudzai that Jimmy had lied to her and that all the other gang members who had moved around with Mary are still alive. She tells Sarudzai the whole story of her life from the time she had left Maruza her husband. Mary says she had joined a gang of which Sarudzai had been a member. Mary had gone to Masasa and stayed with a man called Kuyana. She bought beer and sold it thus making a lot of money out of this trade. The other gang members became jealous of Mary and provoked her to fight them. Mary beat them all up, then left Kuyana, taking all the beer profits with her.

Mary met another man Pasipamire and lived with him in a squatter area in Harare. She sold meat, beer and cigarettes which brought her a lot of money. She carried on this trade until she met one of the old gang members, Jimmy, who told her that the people Mary had beaten up had died. These people were Mai Masasa, Sarudzai and John Madaka. Alarmed, Mary decided to leave for a different part of town where she was not likely to meet Jimmy. She was afraid that Jimmy would report to the police or that somebody who was at the scene of the fight might set the law on her. She left Pasipamire and informed him that she was moving to Gatooma. She took all their money with her and warned him not to attempt to pursue her since she would beat him up if he did.

Mary banked the money and moved on to Hunyani. She worked as a domestic for the people who gave her accommodation but did not pay her any money for the work she did. She was then set up by the man and woman of the house. The woman, Maidei, accused her of having an affair with her husband. Mary beat up both of them and got all the pay due to her from Maidei. She then went to a farm to work. After telling her story, she resolves to continue to work and face life head-on.

In Mungoshi's story 'Some Kinds of Wounds' the woman comes into town to look for a boyfriend who has fled the regime's army. She is picked up by Kute, a young man who clearly intends to sleep with her. She is unkempt, dusty and smells ' . . . a mixture of human sweat and soil and grass and leaves . . . '[5] She wants a place to spend the night and the following day she intends to start looking for her boyfriend in Highfield. She does not know his address since the boyfriend had left in a hurry before he could tell her. She is pregnant and has had her parents shot by the army. Kute has sex with her and then refuses to let her spend the night in his room. He complains that she stinks and will not accept any money. Kute throws her out into the street. "I . . . put her on the street and pointed east, south, north and west and told her this was all Highfield," Kute says. He does not know where she went to ' . . . She just walked straight away from me without looking back—as if she knew where she was going . . . ' The woman is self-possessed despite the desperate situation she is in. She gives the impression that she has been through worse situations and the encounter with Kute does not warrant any fear of self-pity. Kute despises her because she is pregnant and has no possibilities for him. She is proud enough to refuse his money even though she needs it so much. Kute lies to himself that all she wanted was a man to look after her till she had had a baby although he does comment that she seemed to be looking for something more important than money and support. This woman does not inspire pity like some of the jilted single women. She is self possessed and more admirable than them in spite of her destitution.

In the last two chapters, the definitions of women as wives and mothers have been shown to impose a lot of constraints to women's self definition. Motherhood and wifehood define women very strongly as their images demonstrate. We therefore need to analyse any difference to those women's self-definition and to the way they are defined by others.

In the case of widows, their continued well being is closely linked to their husbands' and childrens' patrilineage. Even when widows stay with sons and daughters, they are still dependent on their deceased husbands' kin for such important issues as the marriage of children. A daughter's *roora* can only be received by her patrilineal relatives, particularly the males such as father's brothers or the daughter's own brothers on her father's side. Muchaneta's mother scandalises her neighbours and relatives by receiving *roora* from Handisumbe for Muchaneta. Lifile's mother gets involved in a fight with Bahle's mother's sister because Bahle is seen around with Lifile's boyfriend Thando. Thando's family are well off and Lifile's mother wants him for a son-in-law because she recognises that she and her daughter would be well-looked after if he married Lifile. Even those women who are involved and implicated in killing their husbands do not do so simply to get rid of troublesome or stressful characters in their lives. They do so in order to marry other men or so that they can depend on other people such as sons. Munhamo is a case in point. She kills her husband in order to marry Zimwai. Muchaneta kills Zikomu so that she can be kept by Matamba and after Matamba she moves off to be kept by other men. Thus the death of a husband does not necessarily free a widow from rights and obligations that are created by marriage. Marriage continues to define what she can do for a living and how she can earn that living. If a woman 'creates' her widowhood, she can still be bound to certain modes of behaviour for the sake of her children and if she remarries, she will still find herself tied to the role of a wife with its accompanying obligations. As long as the woman has not independent way of earning a living, her widowhood will still impose wifely obligations on her.

With regard to divorced women, the terminology used to denote their status points to the link and dependence they still have to their husbands. The wives who are divorced by their husbands do not choose their status. It is 'created' for them by their husbands. They usually try by all means to stay married. They may lie or fight to keep the husband and the marriage intact. They try to have children, to cook well and generally do all the things that may please their husbands. The wives realise the hardship involved in being divorced and may opt to stay in a difficult marriage. Like widowed women, divorced women in the literature are very dependent on husbands or male kin. They usually change dependency on a husband to dependency on a brother or father. Rudo, the social worker in *Ziva Kwawakabva* opts to stay on as Ngoni's wife despite the restrictive conditions Ngoni has placed on her, namely that all her salary be banked in his account and that he lays down the law in their home. Despite the fact that Rudo is capable of living life on her own without depending on Ngoni materially, she opts to stay under his restrictive conditions. A lot of men in the literature would not marry a divorced woman. Jane is shunned by Timothy simply because she had been Simon's girlfriend, not even a lover. Zimwai does not marry Munhamo because she is a widow and has had children. He prefers Munhamo's daughter who is young, eligible and a virgin.

Single women also find themselves being defined by marriage or relationships to men. Only those women with schooling or skills manage to go against the society's norms and values that define women's behaviour. Lifile, Muchaneta and Nomalanga all move from one man to another. They do not work or earn their own living independently of or jointly with their men. Without their men, they cannot survive in town. Their freedom only extends to determining which men will keep them. Their choice of men is confined to those men who are willing to keep them in clothes, food and drink. They do not have the freedom not to choose any man or anybody else to depend on for their basic necessities. The only commodity they can offer is sex which the men accept with impunity and then go off to marry or resume relationships with 'virtuous' and decent women. Decent women are those women who do not go from one man to the next with equal impunity.

The single women who have never been married are preoccupied with finding men to marry. They are not interested in relationships with men outside marriage because of the social difficulties and stigma accompanying such relationships. For example, Jane gets so desperate that she risks acting in an uncustomary fashion by going to Simon's house in Harare. She acts in an equally uncustomary manner for a woman by staying with Timothy. Thus she may be single but this is not by choice or design. Her status is one that she is eager to shed as quickly as she can. Bahle also tries to get married to Thando because she realises that there is more status in marriage than out of it.

Jane, Rudo Moyo, Anatoria Tichafa and Thandiwe 'give' their boyfriends sex on the understanding that their men will offer them marriage. When marriage is not forthcoming, the women are devastated and they react drastically. Jane and Anatoria commit suicide when they realise that they have been betrayed by their lovers. They actually let their relationships with their men define their physical existence as if to say 'If you will not have me, I will not be'. They do not love themselves enough to justify their own existence in spite of the shame and embarrassment they would suffer as single women. Jane does not even give her child the right to live as Anatoria does. Thandiwe reacts by trying to abandon her child to start life afresh and probably increase her chances of marriage and survival. She is caught and gets a criminal record which blights her life and that of her child more definitely. Her betrayal by her lover does not free her enough to disregard social conventions and struggle to give her child a better and unbetrayed future. Rudo Moyo emerges bloody but unbowed. She has had a miscarriage and realised that she has misjudged a man to her own detriment. Her guardian prays that she gets a trustworthy, Christian man as her mother desired. Rudo says regrets do not help and she wises she had known people's true nature. She does not look back and she gives us the feeling that she is more careful and wise about assessing people. To some extent, she is the woman who has been freed and educated by her experience. She is more capable of defining what she expects and is willing to stand for in life in general and in a husband in particular. Her options are not yet defined by wifehood or motherhood and she is in a position to redefine them.

Nhlokotshiyane gets her way with her father on the issue of the husband to marry. She has used her education and economic independence to free herself from her father's demands and expectations. Her father does not consult her on the subject but merely tells her who her husband is to be. She respects her father but refuses to let him impose himself and his values on her. She is willing to live her own life as a disowned daughter without necessarily throwing herself at her boyfriend. She does not live with him but buys her own house and continues working. She still continues her relationship with her boyfriend. She takes her own freedom and finally convinces her father about the rightness of her standpoint and the importance of having the freedom to define one's own life and circumstances as far as possible. She is able to do this because she is independent and does not need to fall back on other people. She wanted marriage but she also wanted to define who to marry. This gives hope in that even within the marriage, she will try to continue to make choises about what was best for her. Thus she is dependent on neither her father nor her boyfriend but on herself.

Martha in *Kunyarara Hakusi Kutaura?* has already been betrayed by the father of her child who refused to marry her. She then turns to Eric on whom she pins all her hopes. Eric leads her a merry dance with his flirtations, affairs and indecisive behaviour towards her. She behaves in a wifely fashion to his relatives, behaviour that Eric decries since he feels that she is pushing his hand by behaving that way. She sees evidence of his faithlessness as early as their engagement day but she tolerates it hoping that he would marry her still. Her bitterness does not motivate her to change her behaviour or alter her expectations of him. She suffers in martyred silence. When Eric is jailed, she resolves to take comfort in her job and still hopes that another man will marry her. Her focus is still on a man. She is already a mother but her relationship with her son is superceded by that between her and her men, actual or expected. Her mention of her job does indicate that she realises the importance of economic independence for herself but one feels that she is still vulnerable to any influence by men she views as potential husbands. Thus motherhood may not be enjoyable for the women characters in these writings unless wifehood accompanies it. Single status is still not valued even by those women who can have material and emotional needs fulfilled with or without marriage.

Soneni who becomes Jojo's wife accepts Jojo as a husband despite his abrupt termination of their relationship when he meets Nomalanga. What is more galling is the fact that Soneni does not even ask for an explanation from Jojo but proceeds to forgive him, hoping that he would not do the same thing again. She is quite willing to hope in ignorance of what caused her initial hopes to be dashed by Jojo. She prefers ignorance and the comfort it offers her to the knowledge that might hurt her even if that knowledge makes her wiser to the circumstances surrounding her relationship to her husband. She thus forecloses an area of self-knowledge and the knowledge of her husband in preference for bliss that is based on ignorance of her husband and ultimately, herself. She does not realise that she is opening herself to abuse in the future because of her ignorance of her husband's motivation towards her. In that respect, she is not free to make informed choices in her marriage since she does not know her husband's motivation.

Vimbai is a more problematic character because of her youth and the fact that she was in a situation she neither comprehended fully nor controlled. She is pushed by her mother on one hand and raped by Zimwai on the other. Her respect and obedience to her mother made her exploitable by Zimwai. Her suicide damns her mother and Zimwai but one cannot disregard the fact that it is Vimbai herself who paid the highest price. She did not want Zimwai and had not indicated whether she wanted anybody to marry her or not. She probably would have married but the biggest crime against her was that she never had the chance to choose any kind of life for herself. The only choice she had was to decide between self-destruction and a disgraced, embarrassed life as a rape victim and unmarried mother, impregnated by some other woman's husband. Vimbai's suicide also helped Munhamo and Zimwai escape responsibility for having foreclosed her options as a human being. If Munhamo and Zimwai had lived, they would have done so with the guilt of having destroyed her life.

In 'The House of Hunger', Nestar, the pregnant schoolgirl, cast out of her school and her home, has no alternative but to turn to prostitution to raise her children and to support herself. Nestar is courageous and scoffs at the idea of suicide. She was in trouble at twelve, without money but did not contemplate doing away with herself. She was, in fact, the one who was hard done by, by her married lover and parents. She had turned to prostitution and acquired a degree of material comfort and no longer needs to struggle hard for her basic needs to be met. She has managed, through her indomitable spirit to use the means available to her to overcome the odds against her. She is a woman with a measure of self-knowledge, without self deception and is worthy of respect for that. Despite the fact that most choices were foreclosed to her at an early age, she managed to exploit the few left. Even if she has to continue to operate as a prostitute, she does so with understanding and can, to some extent, define the terms on which she will prostitute herself. She is not so desperately poor as to go with any and every man but she is still caught up in prostitution because of her lack of other skills and her reputation as the queen of whores in town. This also traps her socially and probably makes her unacceptable other than as a prostitute of whom 'decent' women and men can disapprove.

Sister Ruth is a tragic figure. As a young woman desiring marriage, her plans are frustrated by Shingirai. Although Bepswa does not adequately explain why she chose to become a nun, Rujeko makes a choice to opt out of society and live a secluded life. Her choice is unusual since most women in her time would aspire to marry and become wives and mothers rather than isolate themselves from family and any possibilities of motherhood and wifehood. Sister Ruth's choice still irks Shingarai who murders her. For Shingirai, if she would not have him, he would not let her exist. In this respect, Shingirai's murder of sister Ruth serves to bring her in line with the other women such as Vimbai, Anatoria and Jane who commit suicide because their expectations for marriage are marred by the actions of men around them.

Sister Ruth is wronged and the reader wonders why she should become a nun since she still loves Themba. Is she simply trying to please her father and herself by marrying neither Taremba nor any other man? Taremba does not benefit by her becoming a nun. Her decision effectively put her out of his reach in a very decisive way. Shingirai does not benefit but neither does she since she still loves Taremba. Her murder diminishes her sacrifice since she loses her life and Taremba while Taremba also loses her finally. The only person who benefits is Shingirai since by becoming a nun, she puts herself out of Taremba's reach and by killing her, he feels satisfied that she has not defied and defeated him. Sister Ruth plays into the hands on Shingirai and dies without having pleased Taremba by marrying him. She allows her decisions to be motivated by Shingirai's and her father's actions. She loses her life without deriving much benefit from her actions and decisions.

Netsai's life has been dogged by difficulties and hers is a tale of woe. Her mother coerces her to go to town to work and the men she meets during the course of her work abuse her. When she makes the decision to procure an abortion and ease her family's and her own circumstances, it backfires on her and lands her in prison. Her acquaintances have managed to get away with abortion but Netsai does not. She fails to manipulate the town environment for her own benefit and to her advantage. Although she is not entirely forgotten and as friendless as she thought, her final reflections portray her as a defeated person. She questions the kind of justice that victimises the injured and exploited but she does not give the impression that she has decided to fight it. Her reflections do not even address her future and what shape it will take in view of her experience with working life and its hazards.

In 'To Keep Him', Mara's life is portrayed as one big fight. She tries to get important information on medicine to keep her boyfriend, Dan, she fights Dan's other girlfriends, she fights loneliness, her mixed feelings about rejection in her struggle to keep Dan. In the end she is defeated because Dan does not want to see her again. The medicine she has obtained cannot even be administered to Dan because he is no longer available. Mara is pitiable and has failed to come to terms with Dan's faults, her dependence on men and how to reconcile the two realities. She falls back on solutions that lie out of her hands and her control. She is starting the futile cycle of dependence again.

Mary Ponderai is the only woman who tells her own story. The other women characters are seen through the eyes of the authors or other, usually more dominant characters. Mary decides what to do with her life after she leaves her husband. She allows herself to be persuaded by her aunt to marry Maruza but when she realises what a big mistake the marriage is, she leaves. She does not waste time feeling sorry for herself. She questions John Madaka's assumption that he would lead their gang. She opts to live with Kunaya, earning her keep by selling beer. When she decides to leave any man, she does not fall back on another man but works her own way through life. By her economic independence, she avoids dependence and subjugation by her men. She is not invulnerable as evidenced by the effect Jimmy's lies have on her. She is worried and disturbed by the news that she had beaten her former friends and caused their deaths. Mary recovers after treatment and we see her tackling life head-on up to the end. She is courageous although one may fault her for running away with the profits she made with Pasipamire. On the whole, she is fair and does not go out of her way to fight people or create trouble unnecessarily. She acts in a way that is atypical of most women such as assaulting her father and the other men like John. Despite all this, Mary commands respect and she epitomises the free woman, that is a woman who is determined to conquer difficulties and solve her problems as far as that is possible. She is not self-pitying or resigned even though she has been treated badly by her husband. This is despite the fact that her activities sometimes tend to be on other side of the law.

The foregoing analysis illustrates that women without husbands are still largely defined by their relations to potential husbands. The widowed women cannot evade the responsibilities of being mothers and daughters-in-law and the divorced women are in roughly the same situation. The single women continue to depend on men, sometimes more so than married or divorced women. Most single women do not even get to enjoy the rights and the benefits accruing to married, divorced or widowed wives. Single women can be abandoned with impunity and the relatives of the men usually do not intervene since there are no legal or socially recognised grounds for doing so. It is up to the women's guardian to do so on her behalf. (The legal situation in Zimbabwe has changed since 1982). The single women in towns, farms or mines are in a more vulnerable situation if they depend entirely on the men they consort with. Even when the women are in wage employment, they do not consider their situation and existence as legitimate and fulfilling. They still continue to define their lives in terms of whether or not they have been able to keep and marry a man. Very few women who are single are satisfied with their situations. Most of them spend their time trying to get a man so that they can be socially legitimised. Their society views single women as unfulfilled and a hazard to established marriages and unions. Thus unless a woman has an independent source of income and living, she is more vulnerable in consensual unions or love affairs than in marriage. This explains why most single women with little or nor skills and education opt for marriage, even if those marriages are unsatisfactory, than for consensual unions which offer fewer material, social and legal safeguards than any marriage. Only those women of all social classes who have skills, education or means of earning an independent living can realise the benefits of living a single life in preference to stressful or unsatisfactory marriages.

Notes to Chapter 3: Women without husbands

1. page 47, *The Underdog and Other Stories*, Mambo Press, 1984
2. page 52, *ibid*
3. page 57, *ibig*
4. page 59, *ibid*
5. page 89, *Some Kinds of Wounds*, Mambo Press, 1980
6. page 95, *ibid*

4

Rural and urban women

The portrayal of women in literature is closely tied to the conceptions the writers have about rural and urban life. S.O. Mlilo views modern urban life as a source of disorganisation and the refrain of *Lifile* points to the view of urban life as a source of death to the idyllic lives of rural people. In *Lifile*, the vision of the future is bleak and characterised by venereal disease reaching the rural areas and daughters being disrespectful to their elders. Strangely enough it is the women who are blamed for the disruption by Mrs Mlilo. The men who impregnate the girls are not significant in the novel. The girls are just described when they run away to towns but their motivation is not clarified. They are then exposed to town ways which corrupt and harm them and in the end, the penitent women come back, broken and disillusioned, to take refuge in the country homes that retain the goodness and moral standards of the past.

Rural women

There is a marked association between women's virtue and a rural, peasant lifestyle. Most of the ideal wives and mothers in the literature are rural women. Tsitsi in *Garandichauya* lives most of her life in a rural area and only goes to town to try and reason with her errant husband. She is contrasted to Muchaneta who lives in Gatooma with Matamba then in Harare with other men. Vida in *Rurimi Inyoka* also lives most of her life in a rural area before and after marrying Simon. She is portrayed as a virtuous woman who weathers the trials and tribulations of a childless marriage.

Soneni, the woman who becomes Jojo's wife after Nomalanga leaves him, is a rural woman. She is simple, straight forward, forgives and argues to marry Jojo without asking many questions. She is portrayed as an uncomplicated, naive character.

Jane is a rural woman who has been jilted by her boyfriend. Simon, the ex-boyfriend lives in town and visits his parents and his wife during holidays. Jane's attempts to seduce Simon in the country and in town fail. Instead she cohibats with Timothy in town. She commits suicide in the rural area in order to express her shame and to atone for embarrassing her family. Thus, Jane's fall takes place in town where the rules of proper behaviour are not respected or observed while her atonement takes place in the rural area. Tsitsi's parting and her denunciation by her husband also takes place in town while her reunion with Matamba takes place in the rural area. The same can be said of Runesu and his wife in Tsodzo's *Tsano*. Runesu scolds and chases away his wife from town and after he has realised the errors of his ways, he resolves to go back to the country to try to get reunited with her and his family.

VaTamai and Masvinyange the parents of Ngoni are illtreated and driven away by Rudo and Ngoni in town. The reunion between Ngoni and his parents takes place at the rural home of Ngoni's parents. Ngoni's confrontation with Rudo takes place in town and has elements of tension which do not augur well for the peaceful coexistence of Rudo and Ngoni in the future.

Nomalanga Jola is an obedient young woman when she meets her boyfriend Jojo in the rural areas. Jojo, the urbanite, is the one who influences Nomalanga to join him in town. When Nomalanga gets to Bulawayo, she gets corrupted and starts drinking beer, carousing and going out with different men. She continues in Harare, Mutare and eventually dies a painful death from stab wounds sustained during a fight with one of the men she had associated with.

There are other rural peasant women who are depicted as having been corrupted and influenced by urban or foreign values. Marujata leaves her married home to live on a farm because of her affair with a wage worker Kurimahufamba. Kurima is the bad influence and he comes from an environment which is not completely rural. On farms, foreign labourers are present and the compound life on the farms is seen as lax, uncontrolled and socially disruptive. The laxity and lack of social control mechanisms is exemplified by Kurima's carryings-on with Marujata. There were no parents or relatives to constrain Kurima's behaviour. His mother's attempts were ineffectual because she did not live on the farm permanently so could not have any long-term influence on Kurima's behaviour. Kurima brought Marujata to his house as a wife without paying *roora* for her or informing his wife Ndaizivei. He could do this on a farm but not in a typical rural area because socially, his kin would not have accepted Marujata or allowed him to bring her to his home without paying *roora* for her.

Mhondiwa's wife in 'The Flood' by Mungoshi, lived with him on a timber plantation where the men were wage workers. The set up was semi-urban and did not resemble a rural village. Mhondiwa was a foreigner and lived on the plantation with his wife and children. Mhondiwa's wife behaved badly and actually indicated that she had cuckolded her husband. Her behaviour resembles that of a town woman as depicted in most of the literature.

Thandiwe in *Ithemba Kalibulali* is impregnated by a teacher at a mission boarding school. She goes off to a cotton farm where she tries to abandon her baby. She is tried and sentenced in an urban court. Her brother and father bring her teacher-boyfriend to justice in a rural village court where some meagre form of compensation to the parents and family of Thandiwe is achieved.

Rudo Moyo grows up on a rural mission station and gets impregnated by Joe in Gwelo. She lives a hard married life in Gwelo and that is where she lets her husband overdose himself with sleeping tablets. She is tried in an urban court and goes back to the rural mission station to start a new, purer life.

In the English stories and novels, rural women are more complex in their portrayal. The mother in Nyamfukudza' story 'Crossing the River' is a rural woman who resolves to leave the rural area during the festive season around Christmas. She refuses to be stuck in the country and hates to be found by her neighbours there on Christmas Day. She braves the rain, the flooded river and the rickety footbridge in order to get to the city. She goes against the usual image of the rural, country-loving peasant woman. She does not necessarily view rural life as idyllic and peaceful. She is willing to embrace the strange, new and foreign life in the city.

Zakeo's mother in 'Who will stop the dark?' struggles to socialise her son into going to school and preparing him to meet the new life that his education will suit him for. She did not go to school herself but she wants her son to do so to prepare for his future which will be different from her own. In 'Some Kinds of Wounds', the young woman has left the rural area in Mount Darwin because of the war. The rural area is no longer peaceful and ordered. It is the source of her problems and has caused her boyfriend to flee before marrying her. She is pregnant and hopes to find him in town so that they can be reunited and married. The situation is reversed here since the city is now the place of refuge from upheaval. However, the young woman is not a prostitute either and she inspires admiration and empathy because of her naivety, innocence and demeanour during Kute's mistreatment of her.

The other rural women such as Shongedzai are honest, faithful and proper wives. Only Munhamo commits adultery and poisons her husband. She does not fit the simple image of the rural women. Other rural women may be depicted as less than ideal in their behaviour as wives and mothers but they do not commit adultery. Adultery is the province of the urban women in most of the Shona and Ndebele writings. Mazvironda is an unkind stepmother but she looks after her husband and is exposed at the end of the book. Her stepson redeems her by treating her well.

MaSibanda is a witch and neglects her husband but her behaviour is explained by the foreign religion she practises. This religion was supposed to have been started by an old woman from Johannesburg who was hated by her sons. Only her daughter cared for her and it was the daughter's husband who brought the old lady, MaMthembu, to Zimbabwe. MaMthembu was also rumoured to be a witch and it was she that passed on the witchcraft to MaSibanda.

VaChingweru, the mother of Tendai and Monica is depicted as a wicked, rural woman. The explanation for her atypical behaviour as a rural woman was that she wanted the sophisticated and affluent life-style which she could see Mujubheki living. Mujubheki, as his name implies, had been a labour migrant in South Africa and had amassed some money, fancy clothes and goods. It was his life-style that influenced VaChingweru to try to get Monica married by Mujubheki.

Thus, rural women are portrayed as simple, innocent and honest unless they have been influenced by urban people and their values. Those rural women who are not ideal mothers or wives are shown to be motivated by urban values that do not conform with rural ones. Even those rural women who may view the city as a place of refuge are depicted as naive and trusting. The woman in 'Some Kinds of Wounds' is evidence of this portrayal while the mother in 'Crossing the River' idealises the city, perhaps, without knowledge of the kinds of problems and demands it places on people.

Urban women

There are two categories of urban women in the literature of Zimbabwe. There are professional or waged women on one hand and unwaged women on the other. The professional women are usually teachers and nurses while the waged women may work in factories and offices. The other category of unwaged women may include women who are housewives, petty traders, women who cohabit with men in casual liaisons, mistresses and prostitutes. It is useful to discuss and analyse the images of these categories of women separately.

Professional and waged women

Most of the professional and waged women work in the town, mission stations or schools. Among the professional women we have characters such as Martha in *Kunyarara Hakusi Kutaura?*, Rudo in *Ziva Kwawakabva*, Anatoria Tichafa in *Pafunge*, Nhlokotshiyane in *Ngitshilo Ngitshilo*, Grace Mpofu in *Akulazulu Emhlabeni*, and the dumb woman in 'A Fresh Start' by Nyamfukudza.

Waged women are represented by such characters as Mara in 'To Keep Him', Tendai in *Makunun'unu Maodzamwoyo*, Netsai in 'The Underdog' and the wife in 'Guilt and Sorrow'. There are other working women who are not waged. Among them are characters such as Mary Ponderai and MaKhumalo in *Ziva Kwawakabva*. Most of the urban women are prostitutes such as Nestar in 'The House of Hunger', Farai in 'Aftermaths', Alice in *Tsano* and Muchaneta in Lifile. Some urban women are characterised as adulterous women such as Grace Mpofu, Lorna, Nomalanga, Ntombi and Peter's mother in 'The House of Hunger'.

It is necessary to analyse the circumstances of the women in urban areas in order to understand how and why they are characterised in this largely negative fashion. Urbanisation in Zimbabwe was characterised by the migration of young adult males into towns, farms and mines. There were very few women in towns then. These were mostly women who had been marginalised by widowhood, childlessness or orphanhood. In towns, there were very few jobs for women. Even domestic work such as cooking, cleaning and child-minding was done by males, mostly of foreign origin. This state of affairs in the economy left the few urban women without many options if they wanted to survive. Some of the women married foreign labourers, went into consensual unions with labour migrants, most of whom had wives in the rural areas. Others simply prostituted themselves if they could not marry or attach themselves to men on any basis. The casual nature of town-based liaisons generated a negative perception of town-based women. Those women who had jobs or professions in towns ran the risk of being labelled as prostitutes especially if they were not married. Labour migrants necessarily consorted with women on a casual basis in towns but they did not allow their wives or daughters to stay in town for long periods at a time. Rural women resented urban women for siphoning money off labour migrants, money that they regarded as necessary for their children's school fees, agricultural implements, clothes and other consumer goods. Thus urban women were resented by rural women and instrumentally associated with by the labour migrants in towns.

With the passage of time and the development of industry in colonial Zimbabwe, an urban population has developed. This population is composed of people born and bred in the towns as well as people who live in towns most of their working lives except for brief spells during holidays or leave periods. Among these people who are urban-born and urbanites by their outlook and lifestyle, are many women in both waged and unwaged jobs. However, the image of women in towns has not kept pace with the social reality of the towns. Urban women who are prostitutes are a minority in towns and yet they are the majority of female characters in literature of Zimbabwe.

Another issue that needs to be addressed is the definition and characterisation of prostitutes. This issue is important because in the general stigmatisation of urban women in literature in Zimbabwe, there are many differences that are blurred in the portrayal of problem women who may be adulterous, promiscuous or casual in their approach to sexual relationships with men. For example, Alice, in Tsodzo's play *Tsano* is described as a prostitute on the cover of the book yet a reading of the play suggests that she was having a sexual relationship with Runesu after ditching Clever because the latter had no money while the former had just won a lot of money at the lottery. Clever still wants Alice as his girlfriend while Alice wants Runesu because he seems to have better financial wherewithal to give her a better life. The father of Runesu calls Alice a prostitute for staying with Runesu while posing as a niece to Runesu. Clever calls Alice a prostitute for attaching herself to Runesu after leaving him. Clever and his friends visit a diviner in order to try to get Alice to return to Clever and leave Runesu. During the consultation, Clever is told that Alice is the source of his bad luck since she is angry with him. Clever states that women are bad and should be called sinners because they never do anything right for their husbands. He says during courtship women are troublesome, once they are married the trouble continues, once the men try to get women to stop their bad habits, the women react by feeding men love portions as if the men were pigs that need fattening. If men are silent, they are cursed with bad luck.

Tsitsi, Runesu's wife, also regards Alice as a prostitute because Alice has an affair with her husband. All the people mentioned above call Alice a prostitute when in fact she is the kind of woman who has affairs with men who can look after her. She lives with them in consensual arrangements and does not entertain any and every man who can pay any price for her sexual favours. Alice cannot be described as a prostitute in the strict sense of the word.

Madima's wife in the same play leaves her husband to stay with another man in a *mapoto*[1] arrangement. Thus the urban women who is dependent on a man for her survival may try to find a man who has more money, a good job or prospects in the same way that women who want marriage size up a potential husband for what he can offer them in the way of affection, security, a good house and life. The man's long term prospects and potential are important to the women.

There is also the point that the word or term, prostitute, is used loosely to describe any woman who behaves in a customarily unconventional manner where her relationships with men in or out of marriage are concerned. Tendai's mother in *Makunun'unu Maodzamwoyo* calls Tendai a prostitute because Tendai lives with her children as a divorced woman.

Unwaged women

Most of the characters who are labelled as prostitutes implicitly or explicitly either by the authors or by other characters are women who sexually entertain men other than their husbands. Here single women may be called prostitutes for sleeping with men before marrying them. Jane in *Rurimi Inyoka* is one such woman. Shongedzai is called a prostitute by Rwandibva, her husband, despite that he has no proof to validate this view. However, among urban women, the term prostitute embraces a wide variety of women ranging from actual prostitutes to single women living in consensual unions with men. Farai in 'Aftermaths' makes love to her brother's old friend who regards her as a prostitute. She wears heavy eye-makeup, has ' . . . big, red, somewhat debauched eyes',[2] her hips sway under a loose, short and flimsy dress. Farai is sexual in the way most women in the literature are not. Only Muchaneta in *Garandichauya* may be likened to her. Farai only sleeps with the narrator in the story but the narrator makes us understand that Farai is a prostitute. Muchaneta lives with one man after another in an arrangement approximating marriage but she is also labelled a prostitute implicitly by the author and the male characters who beat and maim her. Nomalanga flits from man to man in consensual arrangements and she is disapproved of by her ex-boyfriends who also regard her as a less than decent woman. Ntombi leaves her husband to spend nights away from home and she is also depicted as less than decent. Lifile also moves from man to man according to her material needs.

From the analyses above, waged and unwaged urban women are not usually depicted as decent women. It is not really the issue whether they are prostitutes in the stricter sense of the word or not but that their portrayal is so consistently negative and uncomplimentary. For example, MaKhumalo, Rudo's mother, is castigated implicitly for dancing and holding hands with her son-in-law, a practice which is despicable given the stress on avoidance in the relationship between mothers-in-law and sons-in-law in Shona and Ndebele culture. Only an urban mother-in-law would behave in that fashion! The better urban women are the ones like Nhlokotshiyane and Dlodlo's wife. Even then, Nhlokotshiyane has disobeyed her father by refusing to marry Mayihlome. The author supports her though. Mungoshi in his story 'The Brother' describes the women in Magufu's house. The men talk vulgarly and their women are vulgar too. Sheila gets drunk and sleeps with a man for the first time, Martha quarrels with other women and her boyfriend Sam. In 'The Underdog', Netsai tries to keep on the straight and narrow but the town eventually catches up with her and she gets arrested for having an abortion. Her friend advises her how to abort her pregnancy. Mara spends her time and money trying to 'catch' Dan with clothes and charms. Even the women in the group in 'The rat-race syndrome' are busy competing with each other, showing off and comparing their material possessions, children and husbands.

On the whole, there are very few, virtuous and upstanding characters among urban women. However, it is necessary to examine another dimension of the portrayal of urban versus rural women. This dimension concerns the resilience of urban and rural women. Are urban women more free and liberated? Are rural women characterised as victims? It is also necessary to explore the implications of such characterisations for the futures of both rural and urban women. The status of the women depends on the skills of the authors in presenting and delineating their characters. Sometimes, the reader is outraged by what the author does to betray a character. There are two relevant cases in this connection. The first one is Muchaneta in *Garandichauya*. Muchaneta is introduced and portrayed as a resourceful and clever woman and yet Chakaipa has no qualms about presenting Muchaneta as having entertained her lover in the same hut in which her husband pretended to be fast asleep. This is just incredible and one feels that Muchaneta would never be that stupid anyway! In his attempt to illustrate Muchaneta's exploits, the author is unfaithful to her and the scene is not at all convincing.

Another instance is in *Akulazulu Emhlabeni* where the author, Sigogo, portrays Grace Mpofu as having been stupid enough to talk on the phone before she knew who was at the other end of the line. Later, Grace is supposed to have gone to a white doctor to request him to help her to abort her pregnancy. In colonial Zimbabwe, very few black women would be naive enough to make such a request to a white doctor and naive Grace certainly is not! To make it worse, the doctors betrays Grace's confidence to her husband. The unethical behaviour of the doctor is not questioned. However, the limit is when the author has Grace believe that the pills given to her are going to help her abort the pregnancy. Instead the pills stabilise and strengthen the foetus. Grace was a nurse and it is inconceivable that she would have been ignorant about drugs or the fact that the pills were not working. The author overstretches both Grace's and the readers credulity. This aspect of the novel is unconvincing and the author particularly fails in this attempt at drawing the character of Grace.

However, apart from unconvincing or simplistic characterisation, we need to examine both rural and urban women's reactions and assessment of situations and the criteria and assessments on which they base their behaviour. This might help to illustrate and explain why they are characterised in particular ways.

Urban women as actors

Urban women are used to make moral points and to illustrate the virtues of living and acting in ways conventionally defined for women. They seldom get away with mischief and they get punished most of the time. This is particularly the case in the Shona and Ndebele novels. Lifile who flees her rural home for town comes back home sterile, an orphan, repentant and homeless. However, Lifile is an unusual and innovative, young and adventurous woman. She runs away from the rural area where she has lived most of her life. Her life had been quite predictable in that she had grown up and was expected to marry Thando. Lifile left all that behind and decided to explore urban life. The author does not bother to explore or sufficiently explain Lifile's motivation. Instead she castigates Lifile implicitly and explicitly for leaving her husband, predictable and traditional life in favour of the unknown and socially disapproved life of the town. The conversations in the novel reiterate the evils of urban life and the foolishness of young women who go to town like men. There is no instance where the motivation for women to go to towns is explored. Lifile's family background offers some clues and possible explanation for her fleeing to town. Lifile's father had died and her mother was a relatively young widow who missed her husband intensely. Lifile's mother wanted Thando, who came from a well-off family, to marry Lifile so that both Lifile and herself would be taken care of materially. Households without men are usually the poorest because there is no wage coming from town or enough labour needed for agricultural labour. It is only when there is enough money to buy seed, fertiliser or to hire labour for ploughing and weeding, that households headed by women can prosper. Lifile's mother had not been inherited by any of her deceased husband's brothers so she was not very well off. In fact, she relied on her own brother to help her out in times of need. Thus Lifile could have hoped to work and support her mother with money. She could also have hoped to meet and marry a wage earner in town so that she could support her mother. Lifile's personal needs for a better and brighter, more exciting life need to be taken into account. If she had married Thando, she would have assured her mother of support but at the same time, Lifile herself would have been doubly beholden and dependent on her husband. For Lifile, it was probably a matter of weighing a familiar dependency as a wife with a widowed, dependent mother against an unknown future that could offer possibilities for a more affluent life with different demands on her. Marrying Thando and supporting her own mother could have presented and imposed some constraint on Lifile's freedom of action within her marriage. She would have had to toe the line very closely as a wife if she wanted her mother's material needs catered for by her husband. It is Lifile's tragedy that town life was too difficult and offered very few alternatives for uneducated, unskilled young women at the beginning of industrialisation and urbanisation in Zimbabwe. However, Lifile's experience was not totally useless. She had shown other young women and her community that there was another world beyond the rural area. Admittedly, that other life was not easy for women but it could not be ignored either.

It is significant to note that Thando eventually marries Sithembile who has been raised in town but whose father had decided to go back to the rural areas in order to escape the evils of town life such as venereal disease, corruption of children, particularly daughters and loss of cultural values. Bahle, Lifile's friend, does not succeed in 'catching' Thando despite the fact that Bahle is a rural young woman who has not been corrupted by town influence. Thus Lifile's family circumstances and her personal assessment of the options open to her lead her to break out of the customarily expected mode of behaviour to try out a new option. That her choice proves disastrous for her personally should not obscure the fact that she was courageous enough to break out of a conventional way of life, albeit temporarily, and set a precedent for other women wishing to create more options for themselves beyond the rural life. Lifile's unconventional behaviour also helped to generate debate and discusison within the community. For some people, Lifile's return in disgrace, helped to reconfirm their beliefs and perceptions about the evil of town life. For a few others, her return set them thinking seriously about the impossibility of separating and sheltering rural and urban life completely each from the other. From this perspective, Lifile is neither a tragic victim nor a totally self-determining person especially at the end of the novel when she has nowhere to go but to her maternal uncle. The author conveys the impression that Lifile brought all these troubles onto herself but the above interpretation reveals that a moralistic retributive stance does not do justice to Lifile and the forces that motivated her behaviour.

Nomalanga Jola in *Ukungazi Kufana Lokufa* is depicted as a pleasure-loving woman who destroys and disrupts the lives of other people around her. She dies a violent death as a result of her dissipated life. However, an interpretation of the novel from Nomalanga's perspective may give a different view. Nomalanga fled her home, because her father had refused to let her marry Jojo on the grounds that Jojo was not a Fengu like the Jola family. Nomalanga refused to be dictated to by her father who wanted to impose his prejudices on her. In this respect Nomalanga is a courageous, young woman who stood up to her father. Her father had no criticism to level at Jojo's character or family so his refusal was unreasonable to Nomalanga.

However, the process of Nomalanga's corruption is not convincing. The author gives the impression that Nomalanga was a decent, upstanding woman even after running away from home to join Jojo. However, the speed with which she starts drinking and entertaining other men is too dramatic to be credible. Furthermore, Jojo does not mistreat her so her motivation for drinking and going with other men is not clear. We are led to believe that MaNdlovu was the source of the negative influence that made Nomalanga change for the worse. This explanation is not convincing either because Nomalanga would presumably have selected like-minded friends and avoided people like MaNdlovu. The alternative would be to assume that Nomalanga already had the makings of loose and debauched women even before she came to live with Jojo. If we accept the latter explanation, then Jojo misjudged Nomalanga as a potential wife and the refusal of Jola to let her marry Jojo becomes superfluous and unnecessary in explaining why Nomalanga ran away from home in the first place. In any case, the reader can ask, legitimately, why did Jojo not follow the customary procedure of informing the Jola family that their daughter had eloped and was staying with him as his wife? This is a ploy used by couples when there are obstacles and difficulties standing in the way of their marriage. This expectation Jojo did not comply with and it raises questions about Jojo's virtue since the author depicts him as an honest man who is taken advantage of by a crafty, flighty, young woman. Nomalanga has no skills beyond those of housewife and it is these skills that she uses in order to live with men who are willing to feed, clothe and shelter her. She becomes their companion and generally tries to satisfy them in order to keep her relationships with them going. Nomalanga does what is best for her to survive and she is able to outwit and manipulate the men she lives with. She is dependent on them and this is the source of her problems since she cannot push them beyond a certain limit. Nomalanga like other women such as Lifile, Muchaneta, Marujata and Senzeni, is not completely independent, liberated or self-reliant. She cannot survive where there are no men to look after her.

However, Nomalanga is not a victim even in her dependent situation. She tries to manipulate her various dependencies and it is when she fails to do this successfully that she meets a violent death at the hands of one of her boyfriends who had kept her previously. Even then, Nomalanga, unlike Soneni, the girlfriend Jojo marries, is more assertive. She does not sit back and accept the portion that people around her dish to her. She struggles to live and interact with her society on terms more satisfactory and acceptable to her. Even when Nomalanga is killed, she inspires some admiration given that she had no education and could not marry in the customary manner because of her father. Nomalanga is depicted as repenting of her sins and life of prostitution while she is critically ill in hospital. She regrets the life she has lived before she dies. This ending is typical of most novels in the vernacular where the women who has refused to live their lives in the conventional manner realise the errors of their ways. It nullifies the struggle of Nomalanga against her father's bigotry and justifies the unfair treatment she has been subjected to. This ending, cast in a retributory vein, implies that society is right and ideal in every sense while discouraging dissent or any source of change or questioning of social norms and values. The author then depicts Nomalanga as the source of social disruption rather than the injured or victimised person.

Nhlokotshiyane in *Ngitshilo Ngitshilo* is a liberated woman who resists her father's bigotry and pressure to get her to marry Mayihlome, a young man with only five years' primary school education. She is a nurse and has already chosen the man she wants to marry. She does not have to resort to dependence on men since she is employed as a wage-earner. The author is sympathetic to her and he highlights the bigotry of her father without denigrating her refusal to knuckle down to her father's wishes. She manages to get her father to reassess his perceptions about the relationship between fathers and daughters and to recognise the social change that is taking place in society.

Ntombi in *Kutheni* is depicted as a scheming and unfaithful woman. However, an analysis of the novel from Ntombi's perspective reveals a different view. Ntombi wanted to marry Ntonga but she knew that her society would not accept a barren woman as a wife, particularly in a monogamous marriage. Ntombi took matters into her own hands by faking pregnancy. She also tried to get her mother to help her to get medicine which would restore her fertility. Ntombi is unfortunate because the old woman who 'tied' her has died before undoing the medicine to allow Ntombi to fall pregnant. Ntonga is supportive of his wife so it is difficult to understand why she mistreats him and feeds him the love potions that make him sick. Again, the explanation for the negative change in Ntombi is a bad friend who introduced her to cinemas, drinking and consorting with other men. Since Ntombi depended on Ntonga, one would have expected that Ntombi would try to have children and stay with her husband.

Ntombi can be faulted for illtreating a good husband but it is also clear that she was trying to preserve her marriage in a society that did not approve of barren women as wives. She actively feeds her husband love portions while indulging in her questionable social life. Although she is divorced by Ntonga, the reader can sympathise with her to some extent because she was trying to survive in a hostile society. However, her mistreatment of Ntonga is not easy to forgive partly because Ntonga is a nice husband. The mistreatment by Ntombi is insufficiently explained or motivated since that the author does not delineate why she was cruel especially when she wanted to keep her husband. One can understand the love portions but not the cruelty of Ntombi since she did not have another man whom she wanted to marry after divorcing Ntonga.

Grace in *Akulazulu Emhlabeni* has already been discussed in connection with the unconvincing manner in which she is depicted. However, Grace is not stupid. She is self-reliant since she is a trained nurse. She is depicted as a querulous, adulterous woman although the author does not clearly show why Grace started having an affair with Moyo, or why she did not care for her husband, Ndebele, who is depicted as a responsible man so there is no motive for Grace's adultery. However, once Grace makes up her mind about leaving her husband, she carries out her side of the bargain with Moyo, her lover. It is Moyo who betrays her since he fails to carry out his promise to divorce his wife. Grace takes her revenge on Moyo by stabbing him when he becomes arrogant and uncaring towards her. The reader may be appalled by her mistreatment of her husband but this is due to a flaw in characterisation since the author has painted Ndebele in a virtuous light that is beyond belief while depicting Grace in an overly negative manner. This kind of characterisation makes Grace's behaviour unconvincing and illogical since there is no basis for it in her relationship with Ndebele.

Grace purposefully acts to get rid of her pregnancy and is betrayed by the white doctor who violates medical ethics by telling her husband about the pregnancy and misleading Grace about the efficacy of the medicine he has given her. Grace serves her jail sentence and tries to find her lover, Moyo. Given that they had parted in a state of conflict, Grace is again depicted as naive enough to think that she can resume her affair with him. However, Grace is a purposeful woman whose mistake was to misjudge her lover's intentions towards her. She learns her mistake and pays dearly for it but at the same time, it is necessary to recognise that she is not the villain she is painted. Her lover and the doctor betray her and they, too, must bear responsibility for their contribution towards the ruination of her life. Grace gains self-knowledge and acquires the ability to recognise that she has been betrayed by her lover. She also realises her errors and does not deceive or pity herself inspite of her desperate plight. It is interesting to note that she retires to Nkayi, a rural area, to lick her wounds and start afresh. Again, the rural life symbolises regeneration and restoration of wholeness after a stressful experience and life in the barren and destructive urban environment.

We need to do the same analysis of the urban women in Shona novels as we did on Ndebele novels. In *Ziva Kwakakabva*, Rudo is liberated, educated and from a wealthy family. She is able to get her own way with Ngoni, her husband. She is depicted as cruel especially to Ngoni's parents. However, it is also fair to point out that Ngoni's own weakness is underplayed by the author and this makes Rudo seem very cruel. Ngoni started neglecting his parents even before meeting Rudo. Ngoni was enamoured of the good, sophisticated life and this led him to start a love affair with and marry Rudo. In Rudo, he saw the means to achieve sophistication and realise his dreams. He actively shared her values and was excited by riches because he had grown up poor. His conception of the civilised and sophisticated life coincided with Rudo's and this is why he chose her as a wife. Thus, Rudo's influence has to be put into perspective because Ngoni himself resembled her in values and outlook. In any case, she could not have stopped him sending his parents money, inviting them to his wedding and generally being nice to them if he had wanted to do so. Rudo's treatment of Ngoni's parents was possible because she knew that Ngoni did not care about them. It is distasteful and in the end, Rudo's freedom is curtailed by Ngoni who resorts to strictness which is extreme to the point of repression. His conception of what constitutes African or Shona culture is repressive, for example, he controls her salary and banks it in his own name. Rudo succumbs to Ngoni's dictates in order to keep her marriage and perhaps in guilt over the way she has treated his parents. On the whole, Rudo is a strong woman who is blind to her husband's weakness regarding his parents. She does recognise the change in her husband after his illness and she adjusts to it in order to safeguard her marriage.

Madima's wife in *Tsano* is depicted as a hard woman for refusing to give Runesu time to pay the remaining half of the rent for the room that he rents from Madima. Later in the play Madima tells Runesu that his wife has left him, alleging that he illtreats her. She is said to be staying with another man in a *mapoto* arrangement in Rusape. She is a strong and self-assured woman who acts decisively when she is convinced she is right. She does not sit and take illtreatment from her husband but leaves him to go to another man. As a housewife, she may not be greatly independent from whichever man she cohabits with but she still chooses to go into a consensual union which she can leave at will. Thus, like Nomalanga, Muchaneta, Marujata and Lifile, she chooses freedom to move rather than security and approval accruing from contracting a conventional marriage. It is also clear that the security in a conventional marriage is forthcoming only as long as the husband values and wants the marriage.

Alice in *Tsano* is also very liberated and relatively free to choose partners. She lives in a consensual union with Runesu when she realises that he can keep her in style. She is very clear about what she wants out of Runesu and manipulates him accordingly. She is called a prostitute by the people who disapprove of her behaviour, namely, Runesu's father, Clever and Tsitsi. This does not bother Alice too much and she asks Clever who she was whoring around with, if not with men. She asks him what that makes him better since he is one of the men she had an affair with.

Martha in *Kunyarara Hakusi Kutaura* has been discussed in the last chapter. She is independent economically but she still remains emotionally dependent on Eric for love and approval. This points to the fact that income and class may not necessarily determine the way women behave and how liberated they are. Martha is better off than most urban women such as Alice, Lifile and Mary Ponderai but she retains her fixation on Eric despite the inconsiderate way in which he treats her. If anything, the waged and professional women may be more likely to sacrifice themselves and ruin their lives to accommodate uncaring men. Examples that spring to mind are women like Anatoria Tichafa, Mara, Rudo, Rudo Moyo, Grace, Netsai and Lorna. The unwaged women are much freer since they do not have much to sacrifice or to threaten men with so their most important consideration is survival rather than responsibility. For this reason, it is the working class, mostly unwaged women who are the most resilient although not the most morally admirable ones. The middle class, waged women still need men as husbands to legitimise their social position in the male dominated urban social order. These are the women who are most devasted when their relationships with men fail. This characteristic they have in common with peasant women such as Vimbai, Jane, Munhamo and Shongedzai. This may be due, partly, to the view held by middle class men, that they are central to their women's lives and partly to the acceptance of this view by middle class women.

Lorna in *Kunyarara Hakusi Kutaura?* goes after Eric, her husband's half-brother. She causes Martha, Eric's girlfriend, a lot of heartache. She has a weak and stupid husband in Paul and she exploits his weakness to pursue Eric. Paul does not realise what is happening until Lorna betrays herself inadvertently. Eric is also attracted to Lorna but she lands him in jail when she falsely cries rape after Paul has found out what had been happening between Lorna and Eric. The weakness of both Eric and Paul contributes to Lorna's demise. She commits suicide rather than live with her shame. In this respect, she is not strong enough to answer for her misdeeds.

Anatoria also commits suicide when she is ditched by her lover because she is pregnant. She is not strong or liberated enough to live as a single mother for herself and her child. She abdicates definition of herself and her hopes to her boyfriend Joe so totally that she denies her daughter her love and presence.

Mary Ponderai is liberated, resilient and willing to work for her living. Her portrayal as a physically powerful gangster is overdone though. This is an unusual image for a working class woman and it is larger than life. It makes it difficult to accept and sympathise with her vulnerability. She beats nearly everybody in sight, namely her husband, father, fellow gangsters and the people who employed her. However,

Mary has her life firmly in her control and she does not shirk work. Even when she cohabits with men, she does not depend on them for her material upkeep but works for herself.

The urban women in the English novels and stories are portrayed in a less stereotypic fashion. There are very few that one can make simple categorical statements about. The role of the Rhodesia Literature Bureau in the promotion of simple, moralistic novels has already been mentioned and it affected the vernacular novels to a large extent. The volumes of short stories that deal with urban women were published after 1980, the year of Independence and they are less stereotypic in their characterisation of women. However, the stories of Makhalisa in *The Underdog* show a different influence which makes the portrayal of women stereotypic in a different way. In the stories 'The Underdog', 'To Keep Him', 'Different Values', 'Baby-snatcher' and 'The Rat-race syndrome', the women all whine about how hard they have been done by in the world. In the 'Underdog', Netsai has been jailed for having a criminal abortion. Town life has no positive experience for Netsai who is molested sexually by her uncle and employer's husband. Netsai is completely powerless against all the forces that impinge on her life. Betty and Janet her friend have their abortions without getting into trouble but Netsai gets caught. The characters speak in a stilted, preachy, unconventional style and the reader cannot help but deduce that the characters are just mouthpieces for the author's own views and beliefs. Janet says 'Bringing a child into this cruel world to suffer not only hunger and diseases, but lack of love and security is worse than for it never to have seen the dawn of life. The kindly child-fostering homes just cannot cope with the number of unwanted babies that daily pour in. In any case, those children also long for ideal homes . . .'.[3] When Netsai asks whether somebody would not tell on Betty who has had yet another abortion, Janet launches into a tirade ' . . . there still is so much self-righteous outrage and cursing concerning the immorality of it all and the punishment that should be meted out. But . . . those who do it . . . to keep enjoying a good life are not punished and will never go to jail because they have the money to extricate themselves from these problems. They will continue to freely roam the streets and enjoy life with the self same carefree irresponsibility. Those are the likes of our friend Betty. It is the desperate cases . . . who . . . suffer more for it. Instead of being sympathetic, people are meting out judgement not in spoonfuls but in ladlefuls. And most of those who make the loudest outcries are the worst sinners themselves'[4]. In the end, Netsai despairs and has no plans for her future and in a Christian vein, thinks that women suffer most and are 'scoffed, scorned and alienated by family, friends and community'[5]. She questions the kind of justice that victimises women but there is not indication that she will do anything to ease her plight through her own actions.

In 'To Keep Him', Mara's situation has been discussed in the last chapter. She resorts to supernatural aids to get Dan's affection and fails to come to grips with the world and environment she lives in. Again, the authorial comment is starkly evident behind the unconversational speeches given by Zodwa on the subject of women's liberation. It is Mara the single woman who is depicted as lonely and desperate. Her apartment is dirty since she has no man to impress. In the end Mara is caught up in her extra-terrestrial remedies for bringing back Dan. She has not come to grips with her life.

In 'Different Values', Clara and Liza moan to each other about their jobs, the mistreatment and abuse of wives by husbands, the unhappiness of most marriages, and the arrest of women purported to be prostitutes. There is nothing cheerful about their conversation.

In 'Baby-snatcher' the plight of a woman who does not have a child after marriage is discussed. She assumes that she is the one who is not fertile while the husband suspects that he cannot father children. He does not tell her of his suspicious until after she has been involved in a criminal adoption of a baby. Only then does he tell her he cannot father a child. Ntombi, the woman in the story is cast as a victim of circumstances because her own family, her husband's family and the public condemned her for a situation that had arisen through no fault of hers.

In 'The Rat-race syndrome' the story starts with the woman's prayer 'O Lord, Help Me'[6]. She feels that her house and furniture are not good enough for the other ladies in her women's group. She feels that the other ladies are comparing her house to theirs and she feels that hers is inferior. The ladies' circle discuss other women, their clothes and characters, children, husbands and jobs. She is also troubled by her critical mother-in-law who has nothing good to say about her, complains about food and does not even thank her daughter-in-law for presents the latter might buy for her. The story ends with the woman thinking about what would happen to her when her husband died without making a will. She resolves to continue to attend the ladies' get together despite the fact that it fuels her feelings of inferiority.

The women in the stories quoted are devoid of spunk or courage. One gets the feeling that they are defeated by life and the problems it visits on them. Three of the women are at least lower middle class, waged women. Two are domestic workers. They have the same depressed, defeated and fatalistic mentality despite their different social classes. Their self-pity is not encouraging at all and they seem to revel in their victim identity without necessarily doing anything much to change that identity for the better. These are definitely not liberated women since they do not attempt to gain control of their lives to any appreciable and significant extent. Besides characters such as Nester or Mary Ponderai, they are pathetic despite the fact that Mary and Nester are unwaged or lowly waged and prostitute women respectively. Makhalisa's women have very little sense of identity individually and they pale besides rural women such as Muchaneta and Marujata.

In Nyamfukudza's story 'Lucia', Lucia is a tomboyish young woman who has a strong sense of herself. She is defeated by womanhood and the pregnancy that results from it. She dies and her father and stepmother move away from the neighbourhood. There is a sense of tragedy in Lucia's end and it is clear that she could not cope with the experience as well as she had coped with and handled the boys she used to play with in the neighbourhood.

In 'Guilt and Sorrow' the wife discovers and strengthens her sense of self after she finds a part time job in a radio play. She gradually stops subjugating herself to her husband's demands and she forces him to accommodate hers. She understands his apprehension while analysing her own loneliness, childlessness and ageing. Her husband gradually mellows and actually grows proud of her. She grows happier too and their relationship improves. This is a sensitive story about a woman undergoing the experience of liberating herself and her husband. The process is not dramatic in terms of the events that take place in her life but it has a lot of importance for the couple, particularly the woman who learns to realise her own needs too.

In 'Aftermaths', Farai meets her late brother's friend. She takes him to a *shebeen*[7] then to her room where they eventually make love. Farai is self-assured, physical, unashamed and unapologetic about herself. She knew that her brother's friend had thought her nice. She wanted the encounter with the man to continue and contrived the situation in such a way that she left with him. Despite the fact that the man is ashamed of being seen hand in hand with a prostitute in his old childhood neighbourhood, Farai has no false modesty and is willing to stand up for what she is.

In 'A Fresh Start', the beautiful dumb girl attracts the schoolteacher. She is fearless, calm and undisturbed by the teacher. He is intrigued by her childlike manner which is quite unself-conscious. She had become dumb after a contact between guerillas and the regime's army during the liberation war. She had been found naked, wandering in the bush, traumatised by some bad experience. It is paradoxical that the war which has robbed her of her power of speech had also liberated the country. She is liberated as a national but imprisoned by her lack of speech. She is like a child in her ways and the teacher desires her although her dumbness makes her more complex than is comfortable.

In 'The House of Hunger' the urban women are quite tough and self assured. The mother prostitutes herself in her home in full view of her son. She does not mind her husband knowing what she does. She is in control of the situation and can handle both her sons and her husband. Julia, the big-breasted woman holds her own with the men. She confronts Harry, the police spy and belittles the man, bringing him to discuss things he did not want to discuss.

Nestar is the successful prostitute who had fallen pregnant at twelve. Cast out by her father and married boyfriend, she had made her way up in the world as a prostitute to white clients who asked her to perform exotic acts on them.

In 'The Transformation of Harry', Ada, Nestar's daughter has a casual understanding with Philip but refuses to go steady with him or to marry him. She prefers to be free to have affairs with men she fancies. She is very self assured and confident.

On the whole, most urban women are not ordinary. They are prostitutes, adulterous disobedient and difficult to control. There are very few who are housewives or who lead ordinary, conventional and socially approved lives. The few are Dlodlo's wife, who is chased away by her husband when he starts an affair with Nomalanga. The other ordinary urban women are the wife in 'Guilt and Sorrow', Nhlokotshiyane in *Ngitshilo Ngitshilo*, Martha in *Kunyarara Hakusi Kutaura?* and the woman in 'The Rat-race syndrome'. Most of the others range from the faintly disreputable to downright whores such as Muchaneta and Nestar.

A comparison of urban and rural women

Rural women are largely portrayed as virtuous and more forgiving, hardworking and stable. Are they less liberated than their urban counterparts? Not necessarily, judging by the problems encountered by the urban women and the different ways in which they analyse and handle their situations and problems. The difference occurs in the arena in which the women choose to struggle for their rights for liberation as wives, sisters, mothers and daughters. Tsitsi chooses to remain single and wait for her husband rather than face life as a divorcee with dependent children. She knows that the status of wife and mother is more respectable than that of divorcee. Thus women like Tsitsi tolerate the existing order and try to manipulate it to their advantage. Tsitsi retains control even after Matamba's return because Matamba is blind. She has both social approval and power within her household. Her changed position may not be dramatic but it certainly changes the terms of relationship between herself and her husband. What is problematic is the question whether she knew Matamba would ever return and what benefit the years she spent waiting for Matamba were to her and her children.

Is Muchaneta, dependent as she is on men and her ability to manipulate them, more liberated than Tsitsi who stays at home, rejected but surviving? Is Muchaneta's life in Harare better than Tsitsi's in the rural area? This question can be answered in many ways and each answer depends on the way the reader understands, agrees or disagrees with Chakaipa's characterisation of the two women.

One could argue that Tsitsi uses the advantages accruing from marriage without necessarily valuing her marriage to Matamba highly. On the other hand, one could also reject the waiting period as unnecessary on the grounds that Tsitsi let life pass her by and stopped herself from exploring other alternatives. Another approach would be to reject both characterisations as inadequate in terms of the options they offer to women in and out of marriage. A woman does not have to be a madonna or an unmitigated whore like Tsitsi and Muchaneta respectively. Both extremes can be rejected as unsatisfactory and constricting since most women are neither, both in towns and rural areas in Zimbabwe.

Soneni who accepts Jojo back without question is naive. In contrast to her, Muchaneta accepts Matamba back after he had married Tsitsi but Muchaneta does so with resentment and she later vents her spleen on him for leaving her in the lurch. Muchaneta is not as naive as Soneni and her reaction is more believable than Soneni's. It is also important to recognise that author's opinions and intentions affect the way women react. Ncube, the creator of Soneni, uses Soneni in the same way that Chakaipa uses Tsitsi. The two virtuous women are used as foils for the bad ones, Nomalanga and Muchaneta.

Jane and Vimbai commit suicide when they find themselves pregnant in socially disapproved circumstances. Constrasted with Nestar who is younger than both of them when she falls pregnant at twelve, Nestar seems courageous and more liberated. However, other views would question whether the right to prostitute oneself is desirable and acceptable as an indicator of liberation. This view stresses the qualitative aspects of life rather than the mere fact of existence or survival. However, suicide may in some circumstances represent a total negation of self rather than an assertion of one's dignity. It is difficult to state categorically what kinds of suicide Vimbai and Jane's were. Vimbai did not want to bear a child as a result of rape by Zimwai. In the absence of abortion as an option, suicide may be interpreted as a choice not to have a child involuntarily. Vimbai can then be seen to have exercised this right. However, one can question how efficacious this right was in comparison with her own right to life and the potential to rectifiy the error or injury against her.

Jane's suicide is more negative since she was ashamed of rejection by Timothy and yet she had slept with him believing that cared for her. He had led her to believe that he loved her so the betrayal was his. He betrayed her and her reaction was misdirected since she harmed herself and her child rather than Timothy. Both women chose to direct their anger, shame and sense of betrayal against themselves and their unborn children rather than against their betrayers. Suicide forecloses the option of surviving to redress the injuries committed against oneself or the possibility of improving the society in such a way that other people similarly injured learn to survive and make such injury preventable.

Runesu's wife Tsitsi is humiliated by her husband and she goes back to his parents to wait for him to regain his senses and come back to her. None of the urban women except Martha ever accepted such insults. This is because most of the urban women have no children to consider in making their decisions. Martha has a child and this might explain her patience with Eric. Grace had children but she also had a profession thus she was more free to come and go as she liked. The women who wait for husbands are usually uneducated and unskilled thus have very little chance of making a reasonable living in town. Thus the two Tsitsi's actually make rational calculations about the best course of action and they choose to wait and struggle within marriage. It is important to note that an errant husband seeking forgiveness is at a disadvantage, thus when he comes back, the terms of relationship with the wife have to be renegotiated. The wife negotiates from a position of strength and virtue while the husband has to concede some rights since he is in the wrong and is negotiating from a position of disadvantage. Shongedzai is able to do this with her husband after he has wronged her. Vida, after falling pregnant, is at an advantage *vis a vis* her husband and her mother-in-law because she has fulfilled the requirement of a proper wife. Her mother-in-law and her husband Simon are shown to have been unfair and wrong in doubting her fertility.

Thus there is no clear-correlation between a free and liberated woman and urban life. Some urban women are more liberated than others. It is difficult to compare rural and urban women in terms of how free and liberated they are because their differing situations place different demands and reactions on them. There are women who are naive in both urban and rural settings. Examples that spring to mind are Immaculate in 'House of Hunger' and Soneni in *Ukungazi Kufana Lokufa* respectively. Liberation is the ability to exploit possibilities in an existing situation and to create them where situations permit. Some rural women may choose to exploit existing possibilities, for example, the two Tsitsi's in *Garandichauya* and *Tsano*, Vida in *Rurimi Inyoka* and Zakeo's mother in 'Who will stop the dark?'. Women who create possibilities are those who refuse to be victimised by situations. Only Thandiwe in *Ithemba Kalibulali*, Jane, Vimbai and Anatoria Tichafa and Makhalisa's women are victims. Other women such as Lifile, Nomalanga, Rudo Moyo and Vida struggle to overcome the odds that they face. Some like Lifile and Nomalanga may fail but they do not get overtaken and engulfed by a victim's mentality. They may realise the errors of their ways too late to help themselves like Nomalanga did but at least they are redeemed by their courage against heavy pressure to conform.

Liberation is also a process which may be slow and imperceptible at times. The wife in 'Guilt and Sorrow' is slowly getting more confident and less depressed since she has a job. Mazvironda and MaDube are liberated by the kindness of their stepchildren. Even though there is no dramatic shift in their lives, they do recognise that they had erred in ill-treating their stepchildren and this is the beginning of a process of re-examination of themselves.

Some urban women are actually more dependent and less liberated than their rural counterparts. Makhalisa's women do not explore options but recite a litany of grievances without renegotiating their situations. Mara tries more of the same remedies that failed to capture Dan. Netsai is a criminal and one wonders how she will fare once she completes serving her sentence. She will have to look for a job with the stigma of being an ex-convict. Her fatalism as a wage-earner does not augur well for a better attitude when she emerges from prison as an ex-convict. The wife in 'The Rat-race syndrome' resumes her visits to the ladies' get-together despite their depressing effects on her. Ntombi, the baby snatcher, will probably take back her husband gratefully despite his non-action to prevent her mental anguish over her childlessness and her criminal adoption of a baby.

Thus even when authors depict their characters in certain stereotypic ways, a reexamination and reinterpretation of stories from the points of view of the women characters, particularly the ones portrayed negatively, may reveal a different view of reality. Simple characters may become more complex while the villainous characters become less so. The negative sides of the positively portrayed characters may become more evident while the analysis of the whole situation is altered.

In the next chapter, the portrayal of women as mothers, wives, prostitutes, adulterers and castrators will be examined from a sociological point of view. It is necessary to explore what versions of reality are being presented and why they are presented as such. The implications of the portrayal of women in certain ways will be examined in terms of the problems they create and the opportunities they present for society's liberation.

Notes to Chapter 4   Rural and urban women

1. *Mapoto*, literally translating 'pots', refers to consensual arrangements whereby a man and a woman cohabit without payment of *roora* or *lobola* (bridewealth). The term *mapoto* is thought to have been coined in reference to women 'beating' pots and utensils without and outside socially recognised and approved marriage. Traditionally, a newly married woman was given a young girl to accompany her and help her with household tasks. The young girl washed the pots and other utensils for the new wife. Only women who cohabited uncustomarily washed pots and dishes themselves since there was nobody socially and customarily assigned to perform this chore for them.
2. page 59, *Aftermaths*, The College Press, 1983.
3. page 37, *The Underdog and Other Stories*, Mambo Press, 1984.
4. page 38, *ibid.*
5. page 43, *ibid.*
6. page 93, *ibid.*
7. a *shebeen* is an illegal liquor-selling outlet where prices are higher than the ones approved for retail outlets. Usually shebeens offer extra entertainment, food, music and may be used for purposes of prostitution by men and women. In Southern Africa, they arose because of the prohibition and inability of blacks to patronise bars during evenings in racially segregated areas. Shebeens were and still are income generators for some people.

5

Conclusion

The images of black women have been explored in the previous chapters. Literature, like other media, perpetuates and depicts a particular and partial view of reality. Through literature people who write portray certain norms, values and customs which they view as important. By the same token, those norms and values that they do not deem valuable or necessary may be denigrated through literature. Which values and norms writers promote depends on their views about social reality. In this connection, the beliefs and motives of particular writers are important in determining how images of protagonists may be depicted. It is clear from the foregoing chapters that literature is ideological. Writing goes beyond just observing and recording objective reality. Observation entails reacting to and interpreting what is being observed. Interpretation involves organising observations in a certain way to accord with the values an observer and writer holds. Thus observation and interpretation are largely subjective.

Since people are socialised into their cultures, what they deem relevant, what they focus on, object to and support in literature depends on their culture's expectations to a large extent. For example, the image of women as mothers and wives in Shona and Ndebele cultures is in accordance with the expected roles of women in those societies. In Shona and Ndebele novels, women who are neither wives nor mothers are explicitly or implicitly denigrated by the authors or the characters they create or both. This is exemplified in Chakaipa's *Garandichauya* whereby the childless status of Muchaneta, which is deliberate, is decried. Her consensual relationships with married and unmarried men are also disapproved of by the author and the characters in the novel. The same can be said of Mlilo's attitude to Lifile's consensual relationships and the subsequent problems she faces because of her promiscuity. In most of the vernacular novels, the aim is to strongly point a moral and to punish those women who transgress the rules of decent behaviour for women who are wives and mothers. Some of these erring women die painful, ghastly and violent deaths. Examples are Muchaneta in *Garandichauya*, Nomalanga in *Ukungazi Kufana Lokufa* and Marujata in *Sara Ugarike*. Others are sentenced to death such as Munhamo in *Ndochema Naani?* There are no cases where women get away with adultery, promiscuity or disobedience without incurring drastic punishment. This is in contrast with men who may suffer some hardship for their wrongdoing but their punishment is not as drastic as that meted out to women. Men have wives to go back to after committing adultery, brutalising their families or deserting them. Those men who do die are not central to the novels most of the time. These men's function is usually to highlight the indecency and evil nature of the central female characters. Cases in point are Zimwai in *Ndochema Naani?* He is sentenced to death but his major purpose is to illustrate and highlight Munhamo's adultery and her evil nature that leads to her daughter, Vimbai's, suicide. Vimbai is a virtuous young woman whose adulterous mother causes her suicide. Handisumbe in *Garandichauya* serves a similar purpose in his relationship to Muchaneta. His major function is to highlight Muchaneta's adultery and he is also used as an instrument of vengeance and destruction of the erring Muchaneta, the unmitigated prostitute without the proverbial heart of gold. Shoti in *Ukungazi Kufana Lokufa* is used to highlight the fickleness of Nomalanga and he is the instrument of her death.

This is not to say that such male characters are used solely to punish erring women. They may also be used for the same purpose to highlight the wrongdoing of other wicked male characters and to act as the instrument of their destruction or to bring them to realise how wrong their ways are. However, the men who are wicked either commit suicide, get injured, fall ill but usually they do not die from the hands of others. An exception is Timothy who is killed by Jane's brother. Other men such as Matamba, in *Garandichauya*, Moyo in *Akulazulu Emhlabeni*, Ndebele in *Ithemba Kalibulali*, Ngoni in *Ziva Kwawakabva* are blinded, injured, fined or taken ill but they do not die. They are accepted back by their wives, chastened but not rejected. It could be argued that this state of affairs accurately reflects social reality. However, reality is only partial since every observer sees only those things he or she is sensitised to see, appreciate or disapprove of. Interpretations of reality differ depending on one's vantage point. For example, if a feminist wrote a novel on the themes like those in *Sara Ugarike*, *Garandichauya* or *Umzenzi Kakhalelwa*, the depiction of the female characters would be different from the way it is done by the present authors. The explanations for the motivation of Muchaneta, Marujata and MaSibanda would be explained differently. Probably the plight of young widows, ambitious women and women married to weak men would be highlighted from an empathetic view point. A good illustration of this point is Makhalisa's short stories, all of which are woman-identified and centred. Netsai who has an abortion is not condemned as Balele is in *Lifile*. Both authors are female but Mlilo's stance is moralistic and punitive of women who transgress the social norms that prescribe celibacy for single women. Makhalisa on the other hand explores the pressures and stresses impinging on a young woman's working life as a way and means of understanding and explaining her choice of abortion as a solution for her predicament and problem. She neither condones nor condemns the abortion but tries to explore the complexity of forces that operate in Netsai's life. Thus the author's standpoint has an effect on how outcomes of certain behaviour are portrayed. In *Lifile*, Balele dies from her abortion while Netsai does not. Netsai gets a prison sentence but her two friends have had abortions and have got away with their crimes. Thus the author's gender does not necessarily determine support or hostility to certain behaviours that are socially condemned.

Ngwenya in *Ngitshilo Ngitshilo*, portrays Nhlokotshiyane, who defies her father, in a positive and empathetic light while Ncube in *Ukungazi Kufana Lokufa* depicts Nomalanga in a negative fashion. Both women have been forbidden to marry the men of their choice by their fathers. Nhlokotshiyane remains stedfast in her virtue and eventually manages to convince her father of the rightness of her stance while Nomalanga, unconvincingly, one might add, is depicted as turning to prostitution and living off men in casual liaisons. Both authors are male but they view women's disobedience to parents and the consequences thereof, in very different ways. Their views depend on the assumptions and ideas they hold about how society should operate and what needs to be done if the norms and values are transgressed. Characterisations also indicate who authors view as culpable when the normally accepted modes of behaviour and interactions are not followed.

Most female authors are concerned about the lives of women, particularly in marriage. Bad and troublesome mothers-in-law feature boldly in novels and stories by women. Mazibuko in *Umzenzi Kakhalelwa*, features a mother-in-law who is a witch and is responsible for her grandchildren's death in infancy. Makhalisa features bad and ungrateful mothers-in-law in her stories 'Baby Snatcher' and 'The Rat-race syndrome' respectively. Mukonoweshuro features a wicked and cruel stepmother-in-law in *Ndakakutadzirei*. These mothers-in-law are particularly cruel to their daughters-in-law. Male authors may also feature mothers-in-law who are a bad influence on their daughters but in most of the instances, evil mothers-in-law to men are an accompaniment to daughters who are evil or adulterous wives. Evil and bad mothers-in-law to men are used to explain and illustrate the correspondingly evil and bad ways of their daughters.

Thus the relationships that authors are sensitised to may mirror author's preoccupations, fears and exaggerations. The threatening relationships may overshadow others that are less so. This leads to the overemphasis of the former and the underplaying of the latter even when both kinds of relationships exist objectively to the same extent. The preoccupation of female authors with mothers-in-law reflects the power that mothers of married sons wield in the families of sons. Thus women's power differs and increases with age and motherhood over sons while men's power is maximal in their role as husbands.

It does not necessarily mean that most women are adulterous wives and domineering mothers or that most women's marital problems result from the activities of mothers-in-law. Sociologically, men may be more adulterous than women in marriage and wives may be bothered more by husbands' activities than those of mothers-in-law. What people feel threatened by and incapable of handling is what they will dwell on and possibly exaggerate. With male authors, in a sexist society such as Zimbabwe, women are generally expected to be subordinate to men particularly in marriage. The prospect and actual situations of women refusing to accept social and sexual subordination provokes violent reaction from both men and women who accept the then existent order as right. The preoccupation with adulterers and prostitutes as the most prevalent types of women in towns in the literature contradicts the reality of town-women's lives. However, the fear of women's sexual and social insubordination results in the bulk of town women being depicted as lax and casual in their relationships with men. The normal and virtuous women in towns are peripheral in the literature of Zimbabwe.

Competition between women

Women in Zimbabwean literature are often depicted in competition with each other. Usually it is wives and mothers-in-law competing for influence and material benefits that the husband and son has. Women in polygamous marriages also compete for their husbands' affection and for benefits for their children. Women who want to marry a man may also compete against each other when the man is married to neither of the women. Single, divorced or widowed women may also compete against the incumbent wife of a man. The relationships where women cooperate with and support each other are those between sisters and those between mothers and daughters.

Examples of wives and mothers-in-law in conflict or competition occur in *Rurimi Inyoka* where Simon's mother and Vida, her daughter-in-law are in conflict because Vida has no children and is the recipient of money and groceries from Simon, in *Ndakakutadzirei* where Mazvironda grudges Shongedzai the time to go and buy packaged, supplementary food for her baby Tongoona, in 'The Rat-race syndrome' where Nene's mother dreads her mother-in-law because the latter is demanding and ungrateful for the material things given to her by Nene's mother, in *Ziva Kwawakabva* where Ngoni's mother hates Ngoni's wife Rudo because she thinks Rudo has managed to monopolise Ngoni's money and affection for herself.

Women in polygynous marriages compete for their husbands' affection. Nhlokotshiyane's mother, Madebe, tries to maintain the favourite status of her daughter with the husband while her co-wives, MaSiwela and MaMkhwananzi are happy when Nhlokotshiyane displeases her father. Single women like Jane try to upset an existing marriage in order to marry the husband. Jane tries to get Simon and Vida to part so that she can marry Simon. Bahle competes with Sithembile to marry Thando in *Lifile*. Mara competes with Dan's other girlfriends for Dan's affection in 'To Keep Him'. Married women may compete between each other if one of them wants to divorce her husband to marry the other woman's husband. Munhamo tries to get Zimwai to divorce his wife so that the can marry her. Zimwai's wife gets to know this too. Similarly, Grace Mpofu tries to get Moyo to divorce his wife and marry her. She fails to do this and is left high and dry when Moyo makes up with his wife. Lorna in *Kunyarara Hakusi Kutaura?* tries to alienate Eric's affections from Martha. Lorna is married to Eric's half-brother but she fancies Eric more than Paul, the half-brother. Muchaneta, while married, starts an affair with Handisumbe, eventually gets him to divorce his wife and marry her. Marujata, a young widow, tries to get Kurima to divorce his wife and marry her. Kurima does not divorce Ndaizivei but lives with both women, one as customarily married wife and the other, Marujata, as common-law wife. In all these encounters, women are in competition and conflict and this may account for men's view of women as adulterous, vicious and hard to manage. The fact that women compete for and have affairs with men who have wives or steady girlfriends may explain why men generally have images of women as loose and adulterous, especially in towns. It leads to men mistrusting both their wives and lovers. Men like Timothy, Simon and Rwandibva actually accuse their girlfriends and wives of being prostitutes even though the women are physically faithful to their boyfriends and husbands. Several characters actually affirm this view as proved by their statements asserting the badness, evil and infidelity of all women. Old Makiwa in 'The Flood' says that women are the death of men, they are destroyers who take everything can from men leaving them vulnerable and useless. The man waiting at the bus stop with Matamba in *Garandichauya* echoes the same sentiments by saying that women have all bad traits found in the world, breaking up homes and lives of men. In fact, most of the novels and stories in Shona and Ndebele, and Mungoshi's in English characterise wives as strong, destructive, castrating and bitchy.

However, the underlying causes of the strength and single mindedness of the women are not fully and sensitively explored, particularly in most of the Shona and Ndebele works. Marechera, Mungoshi, Makhalisa and Nyamfukudza, writing in English, are able to do the portrayal more sensitively. This reflects the difference in the development of literary forms in English and the vernacular in Zimbabwe. The writers in English were able to tap and have access to other writings in English within and outside the country before Independence. Marechera, Mungoshi and Nyamfukudza were already published by 1980. Makhalisa had written in Ndebele during the colonial period. Most of the Shona and Ndebele writers did not have much exposure to writing by other blacks in Shona and Ndebele. The Rhodesia Literature Bureau had a monopoly of vernacular publishing and it pushed the simplistic, moralistic novels that did not differ markedly in style, form and content. Thus vernacular literature was in-bred and did not develop much sinse the line of writing pushed by the Bureau restricted the themes, topics and issues that could be written about. Anything vaguely political and likely to generate debate and questioning of the colonial order was suppressed.

Thus, the general repression of literature that touched on socio-economic and political issues likely to disturb the colonial order also had repercussions on the portrayal of black women's images in literature. Women in the colonial era were viewed as subordinate to men. White women were viewed as subordinate to white men and superior to all blacks. Black women tended to be measured against white women. For example, Chakaipa's description of Muchaneta reveals the acceptance of white standards of beauty as the norm against which black women had to be measured. Muchaneta is described as being so beautiful that Handisumbe did not believe that she was a black woman. He thought she was a white woman until she asked for bread and sugar in Shona. Muchaneta herself is depicted as seeing herself as more beautiful than any other woman except for a few white women. If she were white, she thinks she would be more beautiful than white women. Whiteness is used by the author and by Muchaneta as the epitome and standard for measuring beauty. Muchaneta is viewed by the author as looking like a suntanned white woman. Even Muchaneta's mother is said to have refused to let her daughter do any work for fear of ruining her beauty. How practical this arrangement could have been given the demand for labour and cost of hiring waged labour is open to question since in most rural areas, people without hired labour have to do all the work themselves.

Ncube in *Ukungazi Kufana Lokufa* likens Nomalanga's straight nose to that of an English woman from Europe. Ndlovu in *Ithemba Kalibulali* likens Thandiwe's nose to that of a European woman in its straightness. Thus the looks of black women were examined and evaluated against the standards of whiteness. Only those black women whose looks approximated those of whites are viewed as beautiful.

The reasons for characterising black women as strong

Black women have had to contend with socio-economic and political circumstances that demanded strength from them. Labour migrancy to towns by men of between sixteen and sixty years of age has meant that rural women have had to cope and make as good a living as possible during men's absence in towns. Agriculture, education of children, the sustenance of men during unemployment, old age, sickness and redundance demand that women be strong enough to cope. There was no benefit or advantage accruing to women who decided to be delicate, feminine, weak and dependent. In fact, dependency, delicacy, weakness and feminity spelled disaster and destruction to black women in Colonial Zimbabwe. Capitalism reorganised black family life in such a way that men's existence was mostly in towns and women's in rural areas. The strength of women in emotional, social and economic spheres is necessary particularly when they have weak husbands who cannot weather the social, economic and political order. For example, Zakeo's mother in 'Who will stop the dark?' realises that her son has to be schooled if he is to fit into the new society with its emphasis on academic certification. The wife in Nyamfukudza's 'Guilt and Sorrow' realises her husband's weakness and its roots and she strives to achieve for herself without necessarily threatening him. Netsai in 'The Underdog' realises how weak and irresponsible her brother is and she resolves to support her family as best as she can. Martha in *Kunyarara Hakusi Kutaura* realises how weak Eric is emotionally and she tolerates his lack of strength. Mary Ponderai is stronger than her husband emotionally and she realises that she cannot spend a lifetime with such a weak man. Ngoni in *Ziva Kwawakabva* is an ungrateful son and his weakness gets blamed on Rudo when in fact his neglect of his parents preceded is affair with Rudo. Thus weak men tend to thrust the image of domineering wives on their women. Authors who live in patrilineal, male-dominated societies like Zimbabwe also share their society's expectation of women and this results in the creation of characters and authorial comments that decry the existence of women who are strong.

Strong women get labelled or accused of being childless, witches or wicked wives who poison or harm their husbands. In towns, women were not acceptable except as prostitutes because colonial society did not view women as equal to men. Culturally, the men from Shona and Ndebele societies did not expect women to be equal to them either although in the rural societies, a large degree of interdependence between men and women was necessary. Thus town women also compete with and are in conflict with their rural counterparts. Rural women resented the women who lived and worked in towns. For example, Ngoni's mother in *Ziva Kwawakabva*, expected Rudo to come to plough in the rural areas rather than work in town. Mai Mashumba and Mai Zipfende decry Jane's behaviour in town and intimate to Timothy that Jane is a prostitute. In *Lifile*, Sithembile's father gets so apprehensive about raising daughters in town that he decides to move back to the rural areas. The women in the country do not think Lifile and Balele are decent since the two young women have been to town.

In *Tsano*, Runesu is misled by Alice, an urban woman, into mistreating his rural wife. Matamba in *Garandichauya* is misled by Muchaneta into cruelty to his wife Tsitsi, who is a virtuous rural woman. Thus the competition between rural and urban women exposes another dimension to the hostility between women in and out of marriage.

Women in cooperation

Mothers and daughters in Zimbabwean literature are supportive of each other. Lifile's mother tries to maintain links with her daughter's boyfriend while Lifile is in town. Anatoria Tichafa counsels her daughter to marry a nice Christian man. Vida's mother in *Kutheni* tries to shield her daughter from pre-marital pregnancy and later to help Ntombi to have a baby in her marriage to Ntonga. Mai Musindo is portrayed as being in league with her mother against Vida, her brother's wife. Similarly, Ntonga's sister is seen to be in league with his mother. MaMthombeni is against Ntonga's wife Ntombi because Ntombi cannot have a baby. Marujata is depicted as being counselled and aided by her mother in poisoning Mukomodera, Marujata's husband. MaKhumalo in *Ziva Kwawakabva* is shown as being in league with her daughter Rudo, in controlling Ngoni. Deliwe in *Umzenzi Kakhalelwa* is shown as being in collaboration with her mother, MaSibanda, in witchcraft. Ntombiyezwe's mother collaborates with her daughter in frustrating Mlalazi's plans not to let Ntombiyezwe go to her husband Ndlalambi before Ndlalambi has gone through a church wedding with Ntombiyezwe. Muchaneta's mother encourages her daughter to flirt with men and to get material goods from them. Thus women's cooperation is viewed negatively and portrayed as furtive, harmful and disadvantageous to men.

Sisters also cooperate with each other wherever possible. In *Makunun'unu Maodzamwoyo*, Monica goes back to her sister Tendai when she is in trouble, desperate and worried. Soneni's sister brings Soneni's letter from Jojo to Soneni so that their parents do not get access to the love letters. Thus women from the same patrilineage and biological parents may also cooperate with each other against outsiders. In the vernacular literature, the cooperative and supportive relationships between women tend to be viewed as being against men as husbands in particular. This is interesting since when women compete, most men are either approving or noncommittal in their capacities as fathers, husbands and sons. This point has already been made in connection with the attitude of sons towards conflicts between mothers and wives of those sons. Men tend to feel threatened by women when women are not in antagonistic relationships to each other.

Modern day women who are strong, cooperative and survivors are depicted in negative terms. They are portrayed as prostitutes, witches and castrators of men. This imagery points to the facts that women in Zimbabwe do not necessarily accede to being oppressed and victimised. When women form supportive alliances with their sisters and mothers, they are trying to change or strengthen their status and situation within and outside marriage. At an ideological level, the fact that women and men see the possibility of women struggling and manipulating the situation in their favour is evidence that society is not very secure or confident in its apportionment of roles and statuses for men and women. It shows that the roles of sexes in society can be redefined and renegotiated since they are not being accepted without question particularly by women. This is encouraging for those men and women who do not view social organisation as immutable, given and ultimately unchangeable.

Problems in the construction of women's images

Women's images as outlined in the previous chapters are problematic from many perspectives. Firstly, there is evidence of the lack of realisation of the context within which society was and still is changing in Zimbabwe. There is very little problematisation of the reasons why the society no longer operates as it used to traditionally. In *Lifile*, the author constantly laments the changes taking place and altering women's behaviour. There is a certain amount of failure to recognise why men do not feel morally bound to marry the women they impregnate, why women flee rural areas to cohabit with men in consensual unions, why children no longer consider their parents' views and rules as law, why the traditional sanctions are no longer as binding to all members of society, why young women get pregnant, abandon babies or procure abortions. This is particularly so in the vernacular literature where the moralistic, nostalgic view of society prevails. In Makhalisa's writing, a view of women as victims prevails. This has its own problems as will be shown later.

There is a certain amount of escapism and idealisation of society before the influence of western norms and values was felt. In *Lifile*, the father of Sithembile relocates his family, from town to the rural area for fear of corruption of his daughters. He is shaken by the prevalence of venereal diseases. This attitude is escapist and ignores the reality and context within which populations in colonial societies operated. Rural and urban areas are interdependent and the men who are labour migrants commute between town and country at weekends, holidays and leave periods. In a society that does not strongly disapprove of male promiscuity and infidelity, labour migrants can spread venereal diseases to their mistresses in towns and their wives in the rural areas. Although the author recognises that within the rural areas themselves, children no longer revere elders as they are supposed to, the link between this process and what is happening in towns is not made clearly.

In *Tsano, Garandichauya, Ukungazi Kufana Lokufa, Sara Ugarike* and other novels, the behaviour of the women is portrayed as purely criminal, deviant and uncustomary. The complex processes that push young widows, divorced women, single women and uneducated women to be casual in their relationships to men are not explored. It is implied that the individual women are morally weak and thus resort to uncustomary relationships with men. There is not much exploration of the strife, jealousy and contempt that prevails in the normal and customarily proper marriages. Where this is hinted at, it is overshadowed by the supposed wickedness and moral laxity of individual women. Any person reading the Shona and Ndebele novels written before 1980 would never guess that the events outlined in the novels occur in a colonial state characterised by violence against blacks socially, economically and politically.

Almost no white people occur or appear in the vernacular works. Those who do are kindly farmers or missionaries who are there to provide jobs and services for the rural population. The labour migrants do not complain about their wages, housing or education. The colonial order is accepted as given and unproblematic. This is so because those writers who were critical or who problematised the colonial order never got published at best, or got harassed and detained at worst.

Even then, the images of women from this genre of literature remain powerful. The books continue to be used in schools, colleges and universities and as general reading for leisure purposes. One cannot ignore their impact, importance and continued influence on what society's view of women and their role ought to be. Doubtless, they have been useful as a basis of literacy development in Zimbabwe but their shortcomings cannot be ignored. Their enforced lack of context where colonialism is concerned is the most glaring shortcoming. However, their view of women accords with some of the attitudes and traditions adapted from the precolonial era. It is in this connection that the consequences and implications of women's images in literature need to be examined. This will help to point out possibilities for change or continuity of such images in future.

Consequences of women's images

The images of women as portrayed in present day literature have several implications for the way women view themselves and are viewed by their society. First of all, the emphasis on the corruption, adultery and immorality of urban women perpetuates the resentment of women in towns as wage labourers, students, housewives and children. It delegitimises the right of women to compete for jobs in the wage sector, places in schools, housing and other services. It is the young single women who are hardest hit because they have very little legitimacy unless they are married. Other rights and freedoms of women are also likely to be infringed upon when women's presence in towns is viewed as illegitimate, problematic and a nuisance. A good example of this attitude was the 1982 round up of women purported to be prostitutes. Women were required to produce certificates of marriage or proof of such if they wanted to be released. Women from all walks of life were subjected to this infringement of their freedom of movement, speech, association and redress simply because unmarried women were viewed as prostitutes. The subsequent amendment of the Vagrancy Act makes it incumbent upon a person to provide proof that they have a legal means of earning a living.

In Gabon in 1985, a similar exercise was undertaken and women purported to be prostitutes were to be given to soldiers in barracks as punishment for practising prostitution. In Gabon, it was stated that foreign women were the major culprits. Here it is evident that the Gabonese government took the view that Gabonese women were too virtuous to be involved in prostitution.

The image of married women as poisoners and murderers of husbands, adulterers and of single women as disobedient daughters, prostitutes and dishonest lovers helps to perpetuate and justify cruelty against them. The prostitutes and other women are battered, verbally abused and deserted by their husbands and lovers. If the view that the women deserve this treatment because they are bad persists, it will not lead to the reassessment of attitudes towards marriage, society and other relationships within it. For example, Timothy felt that he could desert Jane and breach his promise to marry her simply by calling her a prostitute. Jane had never slept with another man before Timothy yet he calls her a prostitute. Rwandibva calls his wife Shongedzai a prostitute, batters her and breaks her arm. This happens despite the fact that Shongedzai is faithful and has never cuckolded her husband. Dr Stuart's behaviour towards Grace is unethical and her lover reneges on his promise to marry her after asking and encouraging her to leave her husband. Moyo despises Grace after she falls pregnant through him and he feels justified in betraying her. Nestar is impregnated by a married lover who refuses to have anything to do with her afterwards. By depicting women as prostitutes, it is easy to rationalise brutalising them. In fact, in some instances, it is quite conceivable that brutalisation of the women occurs prior to their developing bad ways. In such cases, labelling the women negatively camouflages and justifies their bad treatment. On the whole, negatively characterising women perpetuates the bad, brutal attitudes and actions towards them.

Similarly, women who are characterised as domineering, bitchy and castrating can comfortably be treated cruelly and exploitatively. Their husbands can safely withold affection and attention from these women because they are strong and apparently self-sufficient in all respects. Zakeo's mother in 'Who will stop the dark?' is a good example. She is treated coldly by her son and her husband's father. Her husband is weak and cannot provide solace for her. She is right and will cope but the price she pays is lack of affection and tenderness from all around her. Nobody feels guilty about denying her any tenderness because she appears so strong. Shongedzai in *Ndakakutadzirei* is also strong in her quiet way. She is abused physically and verbally by her husband and her stepmother-in-law. She forgives Rwandibva and goes back to him when he needs her in the end. Mangazva's mother has a weak son and husband and has to run the family. She does not get any sympathy from any quarter. She copes but is unloved. In 'Guilt and Sorrow' the wife acts as her husband's sounding board. She has to accommodate his weakness. When she feels vulnerable and in need of loving and tenderness, she has only herself to turn to. She feels sorry for herself while having to cope with her husband's insecurity now that she has found a part-time job.

The expectation that women's place is in the rural home or in the kitchen in the urban home results from the depiction of urban women as lacking in virtue. Working women outside the home are characterised as insubordinate and difficult to control. This image causes many husbands and parents to shelter women as wives and daughters from other spheres of life. Some husbands in Zimbabwe will not let their wives work in waged jobs. Other families like that of Sithembiso in *Lifile* will seclude children, particularly daughters in rural areas. This encourages parochialism in the women and the inability to utilise chances in professional fields such as teaching and nursing when the schools are located in urban areas. What is ignored is the question of whether one sex migration to towns is the ideal demographic and social state of affairs. For example, the rural life is idealised and yet its poverty, hardship and underdevelopment of rural people is ignored. The lack of safe water, services and comfort is not explored. Women, the major population in rural areas suffer all these hardships. In towns, men also lack the company and consistent affection and relationships with their wives. As labour migrants, they live in very crowded and low quality accommodation, do menial and demoralising jobs for low wages. The division and location of men and women in towns and country respectively does not solve the problems of infidelity, prostitution, unstable family life and alienation. Thus the encouragement of separation of men and women does not solve most social problems. It might, in fact fuel them since women would commit adultery with those few men in the rural areas while men consorted with prostitutes in towns.

Women may also feel guilty and apologetic once they behave out of the expectations imposed by the images of women as outlined in literature. They may aim for the more commonplace, unthreatening and acceptable jobs, roles and professions. Most women become teachers or nurses since these are nurturing and expected roles and jobs. In the literature, there are not women in high and powerful positions within the civil service, the business or professional sectors. The strong women are prostitutes, gangsters and disobedient wives or daughters. It is also conceivable that women may choose marriage rather than careers for fear that if they choose careers they will not find men to marry them or get social approval. The negative portrayal of career women who are nurses or teachers such as Anatoria, Martha and Grace may discourage and inculcate guilt or insecurity in those women who want to have careers, marriage or both. On one hand, career women have money, material goods and the potential to decide what they want and on the other hand they are viewed as insubordinate, troublesome and unconventional in their behaviour. This may confuse and frustrate young women who still have to make a choice while encouraging young men to expect subordination and obedience from women without jobs and careers, whom they may choose to marry as wives. If women have both careers and marriage, they may feel guilty and apologetic. They may feel they have to atone or show gratitude to their husbands for being 'allowed' to have both. The type of atonement may be in the form of excessive obedience that may allow men to take advantage of the women. Thus women's right to work may be endangered if women's role, as characterised in literature, is defined as that of wife and mother within the home. This applies in urban areas since in rural areas, women are the main workers in agriculture thus cannot 'choose' not to work in order to earn their subsistence.

Women as victims

While it is clear that women have been portrayed negatively as adulterous, prostitutes, domineering and evil, it is necessary, in the process of contesting this negative imagery, not to veer to the other extreme whereby women are considered as victims of society and men. This kind of view would overestimate society and men's power over women. The works examined here have indicated that the writers do not feel that the present roles and expectations of women are sufficiently well defined and enforced. Women who manage to poison, cuckold, lie and deceive their husbands cannot be characterised as total victims. Rather, it is more constructive to consider what women do to redress what they view as injuries and oppressions in society depending on the circumstances of particular groups of women in society. The previous chapter did consider the different ways in which rural and urban, married and single, divorced and widowed women manipulate society in order to maximise advantages to themselves. It is obvious that the strategies used by different categories of women are different because the situations of women in and outside marriage are not the same. However, in the context of the western women's liberation movement, some schools of thought have tended to emphasise the oppressed status of women in capitalist societies all over the world. This view runs the risk of being simplistic and stereotypic if it does not specify the circumstances under which different groups of women suffer particular oppressions. It is necessary to avoid depicting women as total victims because it is unfair to those women who triumph against victimisation and those men who are victimised in society according to other criteria such as race and class.

The analysis of women as mothers, wives, daughters, girlfriends and other roles has shown that these women struggle to maximise their own advantages in varying ways. They cannot all be categorised as equally oppressed since some have more power as mothers-in-law, sisters-in-law etc. Accepting a victim status may lead women to overestimate the power of the system against them thus underestimating their potential for struggle to change and liberate themselves and their society. Depicting women universally as victims may obscure the complexity of women's experiences and struggles in pre-colonial, colonial and post-colonial societies. In the image of women as aspiring to motherhood above all else, a seemingly victimised woman like Thandi in *Ithemba Kalibulali* undercuts this image by abandoning her baby. If all women aspire to be mothers as outlined in the 'maternal instinct' construct, how does one explain Muchaneta and Ntombi 'tying' their wombs because they do not want children? If women are meant to be faithful and indeed are created thus, how does one explain the abundance of adulterous wives in the Shona, Ndebele and English writings? This shows that images are socially constructed and are continually reconstructed, struggled against, reinforced and renegotiated. If the society's culture lays down certain behavioural expectations, it does not mean that these behaviours cannot be questioned or renegotiated.

Sociologically, it has already been stated that images of women reflect the values and norms held by the image makers. The images are not immutable and it is up to writers and people who contest the images to redefine them in ways that they deem to be more realistic, constructive and liberating to the society in question.

Bibliography

Shona works

BEPSWA, Kenneth *Ndakamuda Dakara Afa*. Mambo Press in association with the Rhodesia Literature Bureau. 1964
CHAKAIPA, Patrick *Pfumo Reropa*. Longman in association with the Rhodesia Literature Bureau, 1966.
CHAKAIPA, Patrick *Garandichauya*. Salisbury. Longman in association with the Literature Bureau, 1981.
HAMANDISHE, Nicholas *Sara Ugarike*. Salisbury. Longman in association with the Rhodesia Literature Bureau, 1975.
KUIMBA, Giles *Rurimi Inyoka*. Gwelo. Mambo Press in association with the Rhodesia Literature Bureau, 1976.
MANDEBVU, Stella *Ndochema Naani?* Salisbury. Longman in association with the Rhodesia Literature Bureau, 1974.
MOYO, Arron *Ziva Kwawakabva*. Salisbury. Longman in association with the Rhodesia Literature Bureau, 1977.
MUKONOWESHURO, Sharai *Ndakakutadzirei*. Salisbury. Longman in association with the Rhodesia Literature Bureau, 1979.
MUNGOSHI, Charles *Kunyarara Hakusi Kutaura?* Harare. Zimbabwe Publishing House, 1983.
MUNGOSHI, Charles *Makunun'unu Maodzamwoyo*. Salisbury. The College Press in association with the Rhodesia Literature Bureau, 1977.
MUTIZE, Kenneth *Mary Ponderai*. Gwelo. Mambo Press in association with the Rhodesia Literature Bureau, 1978.
TSODZO, Thompson *Pafunge*. Salisbury. Longman in association with the Rhodesia Literature Bureau, 1980.
TSODZO, Thompson *Tsano*. Gweru. Mambo Press in association with the Literature Bureau, 1982.

Ndebele works

KHIYAZA, Geshom *Ngiphilelani*. Gwelo. Mambo Press in association with the Rhodesia Literature Bureau, 1978.
MASIYE, Agrippa *Wangithengisela Umntanakhe*. Gwelo. Mambo Press in association with the Rhodesia Literature Bureau, 1974.

MAZIBUKO, Lenah *Umzenzi Kakhalelwa*. Harare, Zimbabwe Publishing House, 1982.
MLILO, S.O. *Lifile*. Gweru. Mambo Press in association with the Literature Bureau, 1982.
MTHETHWA, Eunice *Kutheni*. Salisbury. The College Press in association with the Literature Bureau, 1982.
NGWENYA, Mthandazo *Ngitshilo Ngitshilo*. Gwelo. Mambo Press in association with the Rhodesia Literature Bureau, 1978.
NCUBE, Nehemia *Ukungazi Kufana Lokufa*. Gwelo. Mambo Press in association with the Rhodesia Literature Bureau, 1973.
NDLOVU, Tommy *Ithemba Kalibulali*. Gwelo. Mambo Press in association with the Rhodesia Literature Bureau, 1973.
SIGOGO, Ndabezinhle *Akulazulu Emhlabeni*. Gwelo. Mambo Press in association with the Rhodesia Literature Bureau, 1974.

English works

MAKHALISA, Barbara *The Underdog and Other Stories*. Gweru. Mambo Press, 1984.
MARECHERA, Dambudzo *The House of Hunger*. (Short stories.) Harare. Zimbabwe Publishing House, 1982.
MUNGOSHI, Charles *Some Kinds of Wounds and other short stories*. Gweru, Mambo Press, 1983.
NYAMFUKUDZA, Stanley *Aftermaths*. (Short stories.) Harare. The College Press, 1983.

Other references

FERGUSON, Mary *Images of Women in Literature*. Boston. Houghton Mifflin Company, 1977.
KAHARI, George *The Novels of Patrick Chakaipa*. Salisbury. Longman in association with the Rhodesia Literature Bureau, 1972.
LITTLE, Kenneth *The Sociology of Urban Women's Image in African Literature*. London. Macmillan Press Ltd, 1980.
MUTISO, G.C. *Socio-political Thought in African Literature*. London. Macmillan Press Ltd, 1974.